Je t'aime

May you always seek truth; and let curiosity be your guide!

— *[signature]*

BETWEEN the WORLD
of TA-NEHISI COATES
and CHRISTIANITY

BETWEEN the WORLD of TA-NEHISI COATES and CHRISTIANITY

Edited by
David Evans
and **Peter Dula**

CASCADE *Books* · Eugene, Oregon

BETWEEN THE WORLD OF TA-NEHISI COATES AND CHRISTIANITY

Copyright © 2018 Wipf and Stock Publishers. All rights reserved. Except for brief quotations in critical publications or reviews, no part of this book may be reproduced in any manner without prior written permission from the publisher. Write: Permissions, Wipf and Stock Publishers, 199 W. 8th Ave., Suite 3, Eugene, OR 97401.

Cascade Books
An Imprint of Wipf and Stock Publishers
199 W. 8th Ave., Suite 3
Eugene, OR 97401

www.wipfandstock.com

PAPERBACK ISBN: 978-1-5326-1944-1
HARDCOVER ISBN: 978-1-4982-4569-2
EBOOK ISBN: 978-1-4982-4568-5

Cataloguing-in-Publication data:

Names: Evans, David, editor. | Dula, Peter, 1970–, editor.

Title: Between the world of Ta-Nehisi Coates and Christianity / edited by David Evans and Peter Dula.

Description: Eugene, OR : Cascade Books, 2018.

Identifiers: ISBN 978-1-5326-1944-1 (paperback) | ISBN 978-1-4982-4569-2 (hardcover) | ISBN 978-1-4982-4568-5 (ebook)

Subjects: LCSH: Coates, Ta-Nehisi. | Race—Religious aspects—Christianity.

Classification: BT205 .B48 2018 (paperback) | BT205 .B48 (ebook)

Manufactured in the U.S.A.   10/22/18

CONTENTS

CONTRIBUTORS

Peter Dula is Professor of Religion and Culture and Chair of the Department of Bible and Religion at Eastern Mennonite University. He is the author of *Cavell, Companionship, and Christian Theology*.

David Evans is Associate Professor of History and Mission and the Director of Cross Cultural Programs at Eastern Mennonite Seminary. His teaching and research focus on the braided identity categories of race, religion, and nation. He has authored several scholarly articles and is a regular contributor to *Bearings Online*, a magazine of the Collegeville Institute.

Jennifer Harvey is Professor of Religion and Faculty Director of the Crew Scholars Program at Drake University. Her teaching and writing focus on encounters of religion and ethics with race, gender, activism, politics, spirituality, justice and any other aspect of social life in which religion decides to "show up." Her greatest passion and longtime work, however, continually return to racial justice and white anti-racism. Dr. Harvey's books include *Dear White Christians: For Those Still Longing for Racial Reconciliation* (Wm. B. Eerdmans) and *Raising White Kids: Bringing Up Children in a Racially Unjust America* (Abingdon Press). She publishes in a variety of academic contexts and public venues including the *New York Times* and the *Huffington Post*.

Vincent Lloyd is Associate Professor of Theology and Religious Studies at Villanova University. His books including *Black Natural Law, Religion of the Field Negro: On Black Secularism and Black Theology*, and the co-edited *Anti-Blackness and Christian Ethics*.

Cheryl J. Sanders is Professor of Christian Ethics at the Howard University School of Divinity and Senior Pastor of the Third Street Church of God in Washington, DC. She is the author of *Ministry at the Margins*; *Saints in Exile*; *Empowerment Ethics for a Liberated People*; and an edited volume, *Living the Intersection*.

Tobin Miller Shearer is an Associate Professor of History at the University of Montana where he also directs the African-American Studies Program. He is the author of *Enter the River: Healing Steps from White Privilege Toward Racial Reconciliation* (Herald Press), *Daily Demonstrators: The Civil Rights Movement in Mennonite Homes and Sanctuaries* (Johns Hopkins), and *Two Weeks Every Summer: Fresh Air Children and the Problem of Race in America* (Cornell).

Reggie Williams is an Associate Professor of Christian Ethics at McCormick Theological Seminary in Chicago. He is the author of *Bonhoeffer's Black Jesus: Harlem Renaissance Theology and an Ethic of Resistance* (Baylor University Press, 2014), which was selected as a Choice Outstanding Title in 2015, in the field of religion. Dr. Williams's research interests include theological anthropology, Christian ethics derived from interpretations of Jesus, race, and black church life. His current book project includes a religious critique of whiteness in the Harlem Renaissance. In addition, he is working on an analysis of the reception of Dietrich Bonhoeffer by theologies of liberation. He is a member of the board of directors of the Society for Christian Ethics, as well as the International Dietrich Bonhoeffer Society.

Joseph Winters is an Assistant Professor at Duke University in the department of Religious Studies with a secondary appointment in African and African American Studies. His interests lie at the intersection of African American religious thought, Black literature, and critical theory. His first book, *Hope Draped in Black: Race, Melancholy, and the Agony of Progress*, examines how black literature and aesthetics contest triumphant accounts of progress and freedom. His next project, *Disturbing Profanity: Hip Hop, Social Death, and the Volatile Sacred*, examines how hip hop culture reimagines traditional conceptions of the sacred and profane.

I

INTRODUCTION

— Peter Dula and David Evans —

Say, who are you that mumbles in the dark?
And who are you that draws your veil across the stars?[1]

Between the world of Coates and Christianity there appears to be the widest difference. Coates's brief comments on Christianity communicate that religion is a subject that is far from his own personal experience. In *Between the World and Me*, Coates professes to no uplifting cosmology, "I have no praise anthems, nor old Negro spirituals. The spirit and soul are the body and brain, which are destructible—that is precisely why they are so precious."[2] Still, Christian audiences from congregations to theological schools engaged the text for its commentary on the state of race relations in the United States. In September 2015, Ta-Nehisi Coates tweeted, "Best thing about #BetweenTheWorldAndMe is watching Christians engage the

1. Langston Hughes, "Let America Be America Again," *The Collected Poems of Langston Hughes,* ed. Arnold Rampersad, et al. (New York: Vintage, 1995), 190.

2. Ta-Nehisi Coates, *Between the World and Me* (New York: Spiegel and Grau, 2015), 103. Subsequent page references will be noted parenthetically in the text.

work. Serious learning experience for me." This volume can be read as a response to that tweet. The authors and editors take it as an invitation to theologians, ethicists and religious studies scholars to engage the book. At the same time, we take it as a challenge to do so in a way that is a learning experience for Coates and for us.

Coates came to fame as a blogger for *The Atlantic*. Beginning in 2008, he sometimes produced ten or more blogposts per week. He also responded directly to comments on his posts, which grew his readership and kept them engaged in his thoughts on the current events of the day, especially as they pertained to racial justice. He wrote on topics that ranged from police brutality, the George Zimmerman trial, the Civil War, Malcolm X and more. He sometimes expanded upon the ideas within these blog entries to make them full articles for *The Atlantic*. Due to his wide readership and some clever marketing, his 2014 article "The Case for Reparations" became his most widely read and acclaimed essay. It seemed as if every major media outlet and anyone casually interested in racial inequity had an opinion on the piece, which made Coates a household name.

His notoriety served him well when he released *Between the World and Me*. Coates had already published his first book, *The Beautiful Struggle*, in 2008, but it went largely unnoticed. His second book was supposed to answer the title of a piece he wrote for a special issue of *The Atlantic* in 2011, "Why Do So Few Blacks Study the Civil War?" However, American racial divisions made evident with the George Zimmerman trial turned Coates's attention away from squarely looking at history. Instead, he began to put history in conversation with the contemporary racial climate in the U.S. Through writing his memoir, studying Civil War history, and investigating Trayvon Martin's story, Coates prepared himself to write powerfully on the problem of anti-black racism in America. Moreover, the readership he gained through his work at *The Atlantic* made it easy to assume that his contribution to the conversation would be significant. Audiences eagerly awaited the release of *Between the World and Me* after Coates's publisher released Advance Reader copies that won a comparison from Toni Morrison between Coates and James Baldwin. She said, "I've been wondering who might fill the intellectual void that plagued me after James Baldwin died. Clearly it is Ta-Nehisi Coates." Morrison's final comment on the book simply stated, "This is required reading."[3]

3. Howard Rambsy II, "The Remarkable Reception of Ta-Nehisi Coates," *African American Review* 49, no. 3 (Fall 2016) 196–204.

Between the World and Me is a letter to Coates's son, Samori, in response to the acquittal of the police officers who killed Michael Brown in
Ferguson in 2014. Samori stayed up late with Coates that night to hear
the verdict. Because he "was young and believed," he, unlike Coates, had
hope of an indictment. When it was announced that there would be none,
Samori said, "I've got to go" and rose and went to his room and began crying. Coates waited a few minutes and followed him. He doesn't attempt to
comfort him or tell him everything will be okay. Instead Coates tells him
what his own parents tried to tell him: "that this is your country, that this
is your world, that this is your body, and you must find some way to live
within the all of it. I tell you now that the question of how one should live
within a black body, within a country lost in the Dream, is the question of
my life, and the pursuit of this question, I have found, ultimately answers
itself" (11–12).

Between the World and Me, then, is not the answer to the question
"how do I live free in this black body?" It is an account of learning to live
with the question. The task of this book is to get us to hear the question and
to begin asking it for ourselves. When we begin to live under that question
mark we will discover, not the answer but that "the greatest reward of this
constant interrogation, of confrontation with the brutality of my country,
is that it has freed me from ghosts and girded me against the sheer terror
of disembodiment" (12). This book is the record of Coates's own journey to
this realization and his attempt to get us to journey with him.

Samori needs this letter because he is young, inexperienced and, until
this evening, sheltered in many ways from the worst. But what about the
rest of us? How does Coates propose to get us to where he is? He acknowledges to his son that "This must seem strange."

> But some time ago I rejected magic in all its forms. This rejection
> was a gift from your grandparents, who never tried to console me
> with ideas of an afterlife and were skeptical of preordained Ameri-
> can glory. In accepting both the chaos of history and the fact of my
> total end, I was freed to truly consider how I wished to live—spe-
> cifically, how do I live free in this black body? (12)

Coates wants to do for Samori what his own parents did for him—immunize him against magic. He does that by not offering him magic to help
dry his tears so he will not be tempted to turn to magic the next time a
police officer is acquitted for the murder of an innocent black man. But the
rest of us, most of us at least, already read the news through the filters of

this magic. Samori needs to be properly educated. The rest of us need to be re-educated. Here in this passage Coates is clear about two forms of magic that Samori needs to be educated away from and we need to be re-educated out of: "ideas of an afterlife and American glory," what Coates calls "the Dream." They are the things that plug our ears from hearing the question.

All of us, but especially "Americans who believe they are white" need this book because, as Jennifer Harvey argues in chapter 4, they need to be awakened from the Dream. "I have seen that dream all my life. It is perfect houses with nice lawns. It is Memorial Day cookouts, block associations, and driveways. The Dream is treehouses and the Cub Scouts. The Dream smells like peppermint but tastes like strawberry shortcake" (11), "unworried boys . . . , pie and pot roast . . . , white fences and green lawns nightly beamed into our television sets" (29). This is the American dream of politicians' and marketers' clichés and TV dramas, suburban home ownership and upward social and economic mobility for all. One problem with the Dream is simply the dubiousness of "for all." Access to the opportunities that might realize the Dream are a product of privilege. Coates would surely agree, but his claim is more radical: "The Dream rests on our backs, the bedding made from our bodies" (12). In other words, it is not that African Americans have been prevented from achieving the Dream by a history of oppression and an endless series of discriminatory policies. It is that the Dream itself is the product of that history.

"Ideas of an afterlife" means just that—life after death, but it may also stand in for religious faith in general. Describing how he survived the violence of the Baltimore streets as a youth, he writes, "I could not retreat, as did so many, into the church and its mysteries. . . . I had no sense that any just God was on my side. . . . My understanding of the universe was physical, and its moral arc bent toward chaos then concluded in a box" (28). At the funeral for his friend, Prince Jones, who is to Coates what Michael Brown is to his son, this becomes clearest. Prince was a committed Christian with an "abiding belief that Jesus was with him" (78). But Coates listens to the sermons and testimonies and calls for forgiveness unmoved. "I have always felt great distance from the grieving rituals of my people. . . . When the assembled mourners bowed their heads in prayer, I was divided from them because I believed that the void would not answer back" (78–79).

Those two forms of magic come together in the person of Barack Obama. In many ways *Between the World and Me* reads like a companion volume to *Dreams of My Father*.[4] Both are coming-of-age stories of young men discovering what it means to be black in America and in the process becoming writers. But Obama's journey leads him to believe in both kinds of magic. When Coates writes, "My understanding of the world was physical, and its moral arc bent toward chaos then concluded in a box" (28) he is alluding to the Theodore Parker line beloved of Martin Luther King Jr., "the arc of the moral universe is long but it bends toward justice" and that Obama had woven into an Oval Office rug. What for King was an eschatological faith claim becomes for Obama an account of U.S. history and the latest mutation of American civil religion. Here is the young Illinois Senator at the 2004 Democratic National Convention. Contrasting his hope with the "blind optimism and willful ignorance" of the Bush administration, he said:

> That's not what I'm talking. I'm talking about something more substantial. It's the hope of slaves sitting around a fire singing freedom songs; the hope of immigrants setting out for distant shores; the hope of a young naval lieutenant bravely patrolling the Mekong Delta; the hope of a millworker's son who dares to defy the odds; the hope of a skinny kid with a funny name who believes that America has a place for him, too. Hope in the face of difficulty, hope in the face of uncertainty, the audacity of hope: In the end, that is God's greatest gift to us, the bedrock of this nation, a belief in things not seen, a belief that there are better days ahead.[5]

Some version of this weaves its way through all of Obama's speeches.[6] Compare Coates: "You must resist the common urge toward the comforting narrative of divine law, toward fairy tales that imply some irrepressible justice. The enslaved were not bricks in your road, and their lives were not chapters in your redemptive history" (70). Here the target is more specific than just Christianity. It is Christianity as it gets caught up in service of liberal progress narratives that undergird American exceptionalism and as they emerged in Obama's intertwining of his story and America's story.

---

4. Obama does not appear in *Between the World and Me* but he has been the frequent subject of some of Coates's finest writing. His Obama essays have been collected and can now be found in *We Were Eight Years in Power: An American Tragedy* (New York: One World, 2017).

5. "Keynote Address at the Democratic National Convention," July 27, 2004. http://www.washingtonpost.com/wp-dyn/articles/A19751-2004Jul27.html.

6. See George Blaustein, "The Obama Speeches," *n+1*, Issue 27 (Winter 2017) 9–20.

For Obama, racism is not essential to the American story, to the Dream. It is not inscribed at the founding. In his version of the story, America is founded on the conviction that all humans are created equal and deserve an equal share of power in governance. American history is the story of making that vision a reality by overcoming the obstacles of slavery and patriarchy. Over and over, Obama offered his own rise from childhood poverty to Harvard Law Review and the Presidency as evidence. He is not just High Priest of the Dream; he is its embodied ratification. Hence, as Coates wrote, Obama "ascribed the country's historical errors more to misunderstanding and the work of a small cabal than to any deliberate malevolence or widespread racism."[7]

As such, Obama takes his place as the latest high-profile representative of the "creedal" or "liberal" reading of U.S. history that descends from Abraham Lincoln, Frederick Douglass, and the early King. Coates represents the radical alternative that descends from Du Bois, Malcolm X, the later King and Critical Race Theory.[8] For the radicals, the American creed of liberty and equality did not exist alongside slavery and the genocidal dispossession of Native Americans; it existed, as it were, on top of it. The latter made the former possible. The liberty and equality of the white community did not exist in spite of the oppression of the nonwhite community but because of it. The material prosperity that is constitutive of the Dream requires the exploitation of those marginalized by it. The nonwhite population hasn't been benignly left out; they have been actively excluded. Moreover, this is not just a fact of the eighteenth and nineteenth centuries, it has been maintained up to the present through housing policy,[9] agricultural policy,[10] and the criminal justice system.[11]

7. Coates, "My President Was Black," *The Atlantic*, Jan/Feb 2017. https://www.the-atlantic.com/magazine/archive/2017/01/my-president-was-black/508793/.

8. The literature on these alternatives is vast. For a brief but helpful recent account, see Aziz Rana, "Race and the American Creed: Recovering Black Radicalism," *n+1*, Issue 24 (Winter 2016) 13–21. Rana develops the theme at greater length and breadth in *Two Faces of American Freedom* (Cambridge, MA: Harvard University Press, 2014). Indispensable historical and theoretical background is collected in Kimberlé Crenshaw, Neil Gotanda, Gary Peller, and Kendall Thomas, eds., *Critical Race Theory: The Key Writings that Formed the Movement* (New York: The New Press, 1995). See especially the "Introduction" (xiii–xxxii) and Gary Peller's "Race-Consciousness" (127–58).

9. Coates, "The Case for Reparations," *The Atlantic*, June 2014.

10. Pete Daniel, *Dispossession: Discrimination Against African American Farmers in the Age of Civil Rights* (Chapel Hill: University of North Carolina Press, 2013).

11. Michelle Alexander, *The New Jim Crow: Mass Incarceration in the Age of Colorblindness* (New York: New Press, 2012).

But if Coates disowns the Christian and American dreams from the beginning, he also has to work through another dream that he finds much more compelling. Inspired by his father, research librarian and Africana book seller and publisher, he spends much of his youth in quest of a heroic black counter-story to the hegemonic white story, "the primordial stuff of our own Dream" (45). His account of his time at Howard University is the story of his awakening from this dream and a stunning and powerful critique of the myths that have tempted the African diaspora—nationalism and *négritude*, for example. He exposes such temptations, or his professors exposed them, as the Dream's negative image. "I had thought that I must mirror the outside world, create a carbon copy of white claims to civilization. It was beginning to occur to me to question the logic of the claim itself" (50).

In contrast to the false hopes and blind faiths of white, black and Christian Dreams, Coates offers questioning.

> . . . I began to see discord, argument, chaos, perhaps even fear, as a kind of power. I was learning to live in the disquiet I felt in Moorland-Spingarn [Howard's library], in the mess of my mind. The gnawing discomfort, the chaos, the intellectual vertigo was not an alarm. It was a beacon.
>
> It began to strike me that the point of my education was a kind of discomfort, was the process that would not award me my own especial Dream but would break all the dreams, all the comforting myths of Africa, of America, and everywhere, and would leave me only with humanity in all its terribleness. (52)

Readers have reacted to the darkness of this vision. Surely, they say, great progress has been made since the Civil Rights movement. Michiko Kakutani's *New York Times* review is representative:

> Sometimes Mr. Coates can sound as though he's ignoring changes that have taken place over the decades, telling his son that "you and I" belong to "that 'below'" in the racial hierarchy of American society: "That was true in 1776. It is true today." He writes that "the plunder of black life was drilled into this country in its infancy and reinforced across its history, so that plunder has become an heirloom, an intelligence, a sentience, a default setting to which, likely to the end of our days, we must invariably return." Such assertions skate over the very real—and still dismally insufficient—progress

that has been made. After all, America has twice elected a black president.[12]

Kakutani's way of phrasing this is instructive because for her, progress, even dismally insufficient progress, is enough to discredit the radical reading of American history and confirm the liberal reading. The implication is that the fact of progress must mean that racism is accidental to, not essential to, American history.[13] But Coates isn't denying that progress has been made. Instead he is saying that mass incarceration, urban poverty, and the murders of Trayvon Martin, Eric Garner, Michael Brown, Philando Castile (and thousands of others, like Prince Jones, not caught on camera), are not just evidence of the dismal insufficiency of progress but reason to rethink the dominance of the liberal reading and the dismissal of the radical reading. Kakutani is resorting to magic to avoid the question, now rephrased as "what if progress has been dismally insufficient because 'the plunder of black life was drilled into this country in its infancy and reinforced across its history'?"

So far it may not seem like this leaves much space for a theological conversation. If Coates represents steely-eyed realism, relentless questioning and perpetual disquiet, and religious people represent fantasy, magic, easy answers and consolation, then what kind of book could this be?

But while Coates's language often suggests such a stark dualism, we think it misrepresents both Coates's position on faith and his account of questioning. There is a striking passage early in the book. After describing the climate of fear and violence of the Baltimore streets of his childhood and the inability of religion or school or the streets themselves to help him understand it, he tells Samori about how his mother began his education as a writer. Any time he was in trouble at school (which was often), his mother assigned an essay responding to questions that forced the young Coates to ask himself why he had done what he had, how he would feel if someone did it to him, what he would do the next time. He describes these assignments as "drawing myself into consciousness" (29). His mother

---

12. "Review: In 'Between the World and Me,' Ta-Nehisi Coates Delivers a Searing Dispatch to His Son," *New York Times*, July 9, 2015. https://www.nytimes.com/2015/07/10/books/review-in-between-the-world-and-me-ta-nehisi-coates-delivers-a-desperate-dispatch-to-his-son.html?mcubz=1&_r=0.

13. The same criticism that Obama made of Jeremiah Wright. See Blaustein, "The Obama Speeches."

was teaching him "how to ruthlessly interrogate the subject that elicited the most sympathy and rationalizing—myself" (29–30).

So we should not be surprised when, toward the end of *Between the World and Me*, Coates turns a quizzical eye on his own relationship to church. In the third and final section of the book, he reaches out to the mother of Prince Jones. Reflecting on his impressions of her, he writes,

> I thought of my own distance from an institution [the black church] that has, so often, been the only support for our people. I often wonder if in that distance I've missed something, some notions of cosmic hope, some wisdom beyond my mean physical perception of the world, something beyond the body, that I might have transmitted to you. I wondered this, at that particular moment because something beyond everything I have ever understood drove Mabel Jones to an exceptional life. (139)

Here Coates demonstrates, for the first time in the book, that he realizes that the church may not necessarily be a retreat or escape. Here it is narrated as the exact opposite, as something that pushed Mabel Jones into the world and not away from it. His encounter with Mrs. Jones also prompts a revision of his early disdain for the Civil Rights movement's nonviolence. Gazing at her reminds him of "the pictures from the sit-ins in the '60s."

> Have you ever looked at those faces? The faces are neither angry, nor sad, nor joyous. They betray almost no emotion. They look out past their tormentors, past us, and focus on something way beyond anything known to me. I think they are fastened to their god, a god whom I cannot know and in whom I do not believe. But, god or not, the armor is all over them, and it is real. (142)

Passages like these help place the apparent dismissiveness of other remarks about God, Christian faith, and the church and, we hope, open up a space for the essays that follow.

Cheryl Sanders's essay, "Echoes from the Mecca and the Capstone," provides insight into the meaning of "the Mecca," one of the more overtly religious terms repeated in the text, and the Capstone. Coates uses both of these terms to describe his experience at Howard University, where Sanders is on the faculty. Sanders describes the formative context that shaped Coates's identity as a part of the people called Black and those who struggle to overcome the plunder of their bodies that fuels the white Dream. She goes on to articulate a vision for a lost black social gospel movement that has been overlooked in favor of a secular black intellectualism, even though

Howard's legacy is indebted to the vision of religious people who made room specifically for Black folk who looked upon religion with suspicion. Her call, then, is to reawaken those religious sensibilities to join with those who struggle, but for her and other Christians, to do so with the principles of Black social Christianity.

Vincent Lloyd's essay "Black Futures and Black Fathers" provides a fascinating close reading of fatherhood in both *Between the World and Me* and *The Beautiful Struggle*. Writing, "Coates does not believe in God, but he does believe in fathers," Lloyd teases out connections and differences between Coates's relationship with his father and his son, all the while pointing out the sometimes frankly religious language Coates uses to describe fatherhood in order to make the argument that Coates's pessimism stems from his secular understanding of paternity. With this understanding, Lloyd claims that the logic of patriarchy and white supremacy are related and offers the wider sociality of the church in response. He agrees with Coates's rejection of optimism, but suggests that a theologically grounded hope is a better alternative than a future based on a secular imagination, be it optimistic or pessimistic.

Jennifer Harvey's essay, "Shall We Awake?," places Coates in conversation with one of the most important recent texts of Black theology, Willie Jennings's *The Christian Imagination*. Despite their differences with regard to the usefulness of theology, Coates's "Dream" and Jennings's "imagination" are two of the most powerful diagnoses of whiteness we have. Harvey brings them together to exhort white Christians to awaken from ignorance of racial injustice, which renders the American Dream a nightmare. She asks white people to view the Dream as a product of diseased imagination and offers Coates's interrogative program as a strategy for waking up.

Coates frequently runs together the Dream, hopefulness, and Christianity. In his essay "The American Nightmare and the Gospel of Plunder" David Evans, a historian of American religion, provides essential historical detail for Coates's assertion. He builds upon Coates's critique of the American Dream to include a critique of evangelical Christian complicity in imagining a prosperous future for white people at the expense of Black and brown bodies.

If Evans reinforces Coates's critique with an account of white Protestantism, Reggie Williams's essay, "What Does He Mean By, 'They Believe They Are White?,'" challenges it via the Black church. He argues that Coates fails to adequately address the place of religion, particularly because religion has been a significant force in the Black struggle for racial justice. While in general agreement with Coates's analysis of the Dream, Williams worries that any critique of white supremacy that excludes the heroic witness of Black Christians squanders an essential resource.

One of the most repeated criticisms of Coates is that *Between the World and Me* is hopeless. The final two essays also take up the theme of hope but instead of repeating the critique, they are more interested in exploring just what is at stake for Coates in rejecting facile resorts to hopefulness. Tobin Miller Shearer's essay, "Hope's Vagaries," does this by placing Coates in conversation with Vincent Harding. Harding, the promoter of hope, and Coates, the commentator on hope, have diverging views on the utility of hope; but Miller Shearer is convinced that beneath that difference is a common commitment to sustaining strength and courage for the ongoing struggle for abolition of racism, for economic justice, for an equitable justice system, and the end of mass incarceration. There is no simplistic way to describe either Harding or Coates, who both recognize the ways in which hope has fueled social transformation and the ways that hope has been coopted to justify plunder.

Joseph Winters's essay, "Between the Tragic and the Unhopeless," presents *Between the World and Me* as a radical argument against national forms of hope, "especially the American dream and the fantasy of progress," a hope that both relies upon and diminishes "the (social) death of black bodies." For Winters, more important than Coates apparent rejection of hope is his exposure of false hope and the ways in which false hope diminishes our capacity to engage in the struggle. Instead of a hopeless ethic, Coates offers an *unhopeless* ethic of struggle, which Winters affirms while also cautiously urging Coates to attend to the festive dimensions of Black striving alongside the tragic.

2

ECHOES FROM THE MECCA
AND THE CAPSTONE

*Christianity and Social Justice
at Howard University*

— CHERYL J. SANDERS —

INTRODUCTION

I am a fan of Ta-Nehisi Coates. I have read both his journalistic work in *The Atlantic* and his *Black Panther* comics. I followed him on Twitter. I have heard him speak at Howard University on two occasions in 2016, as our Charter Day speaker and as a panelist after the November presidential election. So I was delighted to be invited to address his relationship with Howard University as described in his best-selling book *Between the World and Me*, set forth as a letter to his adolescent son, Samori. The title of my essay, "Echoes from the Mecca and the Capstone: Christianity and Social Justice at Howard University" signals my intention to highlight how key ideas and experiences from the book resonate with my own insights as a professor of Christian ethics teaching at Howard University for more than three decades. I will frame my responses to Coates's thought in terms of two distinctive institutional identities that come into play in his portrayals of Howard University: The Mecca and The Capstone. In *Between the World and Me*, Coates's preferred nomenclature for Howard University is The Mecca, with special emphasis upon "the warmth of dark energies" he experienced there. The Howard University known as The Capstone has an ethical tradition, mission and impact deeply rooted in its historic role as purveyor of the black social gospel. Coates was admitted to The Capstone, but he revels in the embrace of The Mecca.

THE MECCA

I begin with the Mecca because of this remarkable declaration Coates makes in his letter to his son when giving an account of his formative years as a student at Howard: "My only Mecca, was, is, and shall always be Howard University."[1] His initial description of the scope of its national influence, its particular prominence among HBCUs and its global impact is introduced with laconic precision:

> I was admitted to Howard University, but formed and shaped by The Mecca. These institutions are related but not the same. Howard University is an institution of higher education, concerned with the LSAT, magna cum laude, and Phi Beta Kappa. The Mecca is a machine, crafted to capture and concentrate the dark energy of all African peoples and inject it directly into the student body. The Mecca derives its power from the heritage of Howard University, which in Jim Crow days enjoyed a near-monopoly on black talent. And whereas most other historically black schools were scattered like forts in the great wilderness of the old Confederacy, Howard was in Washington, D.C.—Chocolate City—and thus in proximity to both federal power and black power. The result was an alumni and professorate that spanned genre and generation—Charles Drew, Amiri Baraka, Thurgood Marshall, Ossie Davis, Doug Wilder, David Dinkins, Lucille Clifton, Toni Morrison, Kwame Ture. The history, the location, the alumni combined to create The Mecca—the crossroads of the black diaspora. (40)

The original Mecca is a city in Saudi Arabia—the birthplace of the prophet Muhammad, the holiest city of Islam, the site of an annual pilgrimage that

1. Ta-Nehisi Coates, *Between the World and Me* (New York: Spiegel & Grau, 2015), 39. Subsequent references will be noted parenthetically in the text.

attracts millions of Muslims from all over the world. It follows that the word "Mecca" is sometimes used in general to refer to a place of pilgrimage, a journey to a place associated with someone or something well known or respected, notably a sacred place or shrine. Mecca can also name a center of activity sought by a group of people with a common interest. For Coates, The Mecca that is Howard has multiple meanings—the power of black diaspora, its position in relation to other schools, its location in the nation's Capitol, the prominence of fellow pilgrims who are Howard alums. The Mecca signifies much more than a nickname for the Howard experience; it is at once a machine, a legacy, a place, a performance of black energy.

As a Christian ethicist, my attention is drawn to two particular episodes in Coates's discourses on The Mecca that elicit theological and ethical reflection, although neither episode makes any explicit reference to Islamic religion or spirituality. First is the story of Prince Jones, a Howard student of Coates's acquaintance who was shot and killed in a Northern Virginia suburb of DC by a Prince George's County (Maryland) police officer who claimed that Jones had tried to run over him with his vehicle. A funeral service was held for Jones at the Howard University Rankin Chapel. Coates attended the funeral, and as he sat he recalled his prior chapel visits, "where I'd once sat amazed at the parade of activists and intellectuals— Joseph Lowery, Cornel West, Calvin Butts—who preached at that pulpit" (77–78). Coates says the president of Howard University stood and wept at the funeral. He notes the people who spoke of Prince's religious zeal as a born-again Christian, his abiding belief that Jesus was with him, his mother speaking of his death as "a call to move from her comfortable suburban life into activism" (78). Coates was unmoved by the appeals of several people to ask forgiveness of the officer who killed Jones: "For the crime of destroying the body of Prince Jones, I did not believe in forgiveness. When the assembled mourners bowed their heads in prayer, I was divided from them because I believed that the void would not answer back" (79). Coates saw no higher purpose in the death of Prince Jones, and no rationale for forgiveness. Instead, against the backdrop of The Mecca, his grief turned to fear and despair: "I thought of all the beautiful black people I'd seen at The Mecca, all their variation, all their hair, all their language, all their stories and geography, all their stunning humanity, and none of it could save them from the mark of plunder and the gravity of our particular world" (81).

Plunder is a word Coates uses throughout the book to name the destruction of black bodies that has occurred with impunity for the purpose of securing the dreams of "people who believe they are white," borrowing a phrase from James Baldwin. A significant ethical claim is made here by Coates, speaking not as a Christian, but on behalf of a Christian whose faith and class and wealth did not exempt him from this death:

> Prince Jones was the superlative of all my fears. And if he, good Christian, scion of a striving class, patron saint of the twice as good, could be forever bound, who then could not? And the plunder was not just of Prince alone. Think of all the love poured into him. Think of the tuitions for Montessori and music lessons. (81)

This portrayal of Prince Jones and the circumstances of his death affected me deeply as I read it for the first time, perhaps because it evoked memories of the music lessons and Montessori education I invested in my own two children. What I read into it was a broader appreciation for the pronouncement that "black lives matter," both the meaning of these words and the movement they have engendered. The particular human face Coates ascribes to yet another case of an unarmed black man shot and killed by a police officer is characterized by faith, friendship, personality, wealth, education, opportunity, and "all the love poured into him" by his family and friends. Too often the victims of fatal police shootings are portrayed as anything but law-abiding citizens, but rather as dangerous individuals, as menaces to society who deserved to die because of their enduring predisposition to criminal behavior. Significantly, Coates is blunt and transparent in his description of the fear and rage he experienced in response to the death of Prince Jones: "The entire episode took me from fear to rage that burned in me then, animates me now, and will likely leave me on fire for the rest of my days. I still had my journalism. My response was, in this moment, to write" (83). This book, then, can be seen as a continuous channeling of that emotion and energy into a zealous journalism. Coates reports that Jones appeared to him supernaturally in some sort of dream or vision:

> I saw Prince Jones, one last time, alive and whole. He was standing in front of me. We were in a museum. I felt in that moment that his death had just been an awful dream. No, a premonition. But I had a chance. I would warn him. I walked over, gave him a pound, and felt that heat of the spectrum, the warmth of The Mecca. I wanted to tell him something. I wanted to say—Beware the plunderer. But when I opened my mouth, he just shook his head and walked away. (87–88)

It seems that Coates felt some sense of consolation as he shared the warmth of the Mecca with his deceased friend, notwithstanding the failure and futility of words. Curiously Coates offers no explanation of how this encounter either contradicted or supported his view that soul, spirit and self have no existence apart from the body, and that there is no life after death. However, while he remains respectful of the born-again faith and generosity of Prince Jones, he also acknowledges with great sadness that after the plunder of his body, the place of warmth he felt for Jones became a wound. The gravity of this lament impels the morally conscientious Christian to reconsider the specific patterns of injustice configured in these incidents before uttering "all lives matter" as a pious pronouncement that denies the fixed racial polarities of plunder.

The second episode at The Mecca that interests me as an ethicist and as a Christian is a much happier encounter: Howard's Homecoming. The account is offered near the end of the book as Coates recalls driving alone after having visited the home of Dr. Mabel Jones, mother of Prince Jones. She had told him that Prince chose Howard over Harvard, Princeton, Yale, Columbia and Stanford, although he was "that caliber of student." Prince was tired of having to "represent" to other people as the only black student in a predominantly white school. Coates notes that like a third of the students who come to Howard, Prince came there "to be normal—and even more, to see how broad the black normal really is" (142). Coates reflects further on all that Prince's mother invested in him, which was now lost, on the loneliness that sent Prince to The Mecca, and that The Mecca could not save him. Here, recall of the "warmth of dark energies" that drew them both to The Mecca revives a recollection of the happy Homecoming. Coates describes his extraordinary experience with "the entire diaspora" during the football game and at the tailgate party that followed, as a healing, liberating moment in the company of hustlers, lawyers, Kappas, busters, doctors, barbers, Deltas, drunkards, geeks and nerds:

> I felt myself disappearing into all of their bodies. The birthmark of damnation faded, and I could feel the weight of my arms and hear the heave in my breath and I was not talking then, because there was no point. There was a moment, a joyous moment, beyond the Dream—a moment imbued by a power more gorgeous than any voting rights bill. This power, this black power, originates in a view of the American galaxy taken from a dark and essential planet. And black power births a kind of understanding that illuminates all the galaxies in their truest colors. (147–49)

His observation is that here is where the "one-drop rule" of Dreamers was flipped: "They made us into a race. We made ourselves into a people. Here at the Mecca, under pain of selection, we have made a home" (149). Notwithstanding the prevailing influence of cognac and beer, this moment of communal exhilaration was what I would call a baptism, an immersion, a transcendent and transformative experience infused with virtues such as forgiveness, joy, triumph, insight and illumination, not only for those drawn to The Mecca, but for the inhabitants of all galaxies. This Homecoming memory professes a culturally authentic, politically relevant black power, outsized in its cosmic proportions. Those who dare to embrace it also experience a rebirth of sight and sensibility that energizes both the plundered and the Dreamers whose dominance and comfort the plunder has sustained.

As the book draws to a close, the happiness evaporates and the cosmic power of black humanity is foreclosed by the resumption of an all too familiar discourse of doom and fear. Importantly, Coates situates his reflections on the coming apocalypse of plunder in the historic tradition of prophetic doom articulated in the African American community by Marcus Garvey and Malcolm X in the last century, and by Dr. Mabel Jones in the conversation that launched his ruminations. From a twenty-first-century vantage point he envisions dire environmental consequences of plunder that have been set in motion by a global economy initially capitalized by the forced labor of slaves:

> It was the cotton that passed through our chained hands that inaugurated this age. It is the flight from us that sent them sprawling into the subdivided woods. And the methods of transport through these new subdivisions, across the sprawl, is the automobile, the noose around the neck of the earth, and ultimately the Dreamers themselves. (151)

Coates confesses to his son his doubts that anything can be done to stop the Dreamers and the consequences of their plunder: "I do not believe that we can stop them, Samori, because they must ultimately stop themselves" (151). Yet, an ethical impact issues from The Mecca's warmth of dark energies and imbuement of black power that fuels the emergence of struggle as a morally defensible response to plunder. Coates's rejection of Christian religion prods him to prefer struggle over the options that would be preferred by Christian ethics—faith, love, and hope. Hence his concluding advice to Samori favors struggle over prayer as a remedy:

Struggle for the memory of your ancestors. Struggle for wisdom. Struggle for the warmth of the Mecca. Struggle for your grandmother and grandfather, for your name. But do not struggle for the Dreamers. Hope for them. Pray for them, if you are so moved. But do not pin your struggle on their conversion. The Dreamers will have to learn to struggle themselves, to understand that the field for their Dream, the stage where they have painted themselves white, is the deathbed of us all. The Dream is the same habit that endangers the planet, the same habit that sees our bodies stowed away in prisons and ghettos. (151)

THE CAPSTONE

While Coates clearly states that his fondest recollections of his experience of Howard are his memories of The Mecca, The Capstone names the university to which he was admitted, where he occasionally attended classes, received vital mentoring and direction in his intellectual pursuits, and in whose libraries he read broadly and voraciously. Many colleges and universities in the U.S., including Howard, were founded by religious organizations with a focus on Christian mission. Some of them have maintained a strong institutional identity as Christian colleges or universities, while others, including Howard, have not. The denominational influence of Howard's Congregationalist forefathers has subsided over the course of a century and a half, and a non-sectarian tradition of *veritas et utilitas*, "truth and service," has been upheld as a motto for an academic community populated by persons of many faiths and no faith. Yet, I would argue that our social vision, teaching and research at Howard University, especially at the School of Divinity, still largely emanate from the same intersections of Christian faith and social justice advocacy that motivated the founders to create a school for training teachers and ministers.

In 1866 members of the First Congregational Church in Washington, DC met to discuss the church's responsibility to address the needs of four million persons who had been freed from slavery by the Emancipation Proclamation and victory of the Union Army. The decision was made to name the school after General Oliver O. Howard, who headed the Freedman's Bureau and was a member of the church. A bill of incorporation was presented to the U.S. Congress in January 1867, and the charter was signed into law by President Andrew Johnson on March 2, 1867. All but three of the original seventeen incorporators were members of First Congregational Church. The first five students admitted were white and female, the daughters of incorporators who served as ministers at First Congregational Church. The normal and preparatory departments offered classes beginning on May 1, 1867, in a building rented from the Freedmen's Bureau. Within the first two years, several departments were established, including law, medicine, rhetoric, English literature, Latin and Greek. The theology department was organized in 1870 under the direction of Reverend John B. Reeve.[2]

In a piece he wrote for the *Washington City Paper* in 1999, Coates notes that this comprehensive model of education set Howard University apart from other historically black schools, for example, Booker T. Washington's Tuskegee Institute, where students were principally taught trade skills. Howard offered a broad range of educational opportunities as well as basic skills. The Capstone came to prominence with the emergence of a cadre of distinguished professors teaching at Howard in the 1920s, including civil rights lawyer Charles Hamilton Houston and philosopher Alain Locke, one of the leading lights of the Harlem Renaissance. Howard's first black president, Mordecai Wyatt Johnson, took office in 1926. He was a Baptist minister who did his undergraduate degree at what is now known as Morehouse College, and graduate studies at Colgate Rochester and Harvard Divinity Schools. In his book, *In Search of the Talented Tenth: Howard University Public Intellectuals and the Dilemmas of Race, 1926–1970*, Zachery Williams commends Johnson's ability to find a balance between multiple roles of black preacher, black religious intellectual, and black public intellectual, all while functioning as an effective and inspiring president.[3] Coates acknowledges the radical political character of Johnson's leadership:

> [I]t was under Mordecai W. Johnson that the Howard mystique came into full bloom, with the school both flourishing intellectually and—as struggles against segregation heated up—serving as a hotbed of political activity. . . During Johnson's reign, every aspect of the campus, from the students up through the administration, was energized. When he left office, in 1960, John F. Kennedy called

---

2. Everett O. Alldredge, "Centennial History of First Congregational Church 1865–1965," http://www.fccuccdc.org/history/history.htm.

3. Zachery R. Williams, *In Search of the Talented Tenth: Howard University Public Intellectuals and the Dilemmas of Race, 1926–1970* (Columbia: University of Missouri Press, 2009), 69.

Johnson one of the greatest educators the nation had seen this century.[4]

To support his claim that Howard was once The Mecca of black American leadership, Coates describes a famous photo taken at Howard University in 1950 depicting a "dream team" of six black intellectuals who taught at Howard during Johnson's presidency: James M. Nabrit Jr., professor of law who succeeded Johnson as president of Howard University; Charles Drew, creator of the first blood-plasma bank; Sterling Brown, internationally renowned poet; E. Franklin Frazier, sociologist and author of *Black Bourgeoisie*; Rayford W. Logan, historian; and Alain Locke. This same photo is featured on the front of the dust jacket of Zachery Williams's book. No theologians or religion scholars are in the picture. A partial explanation can be found in *The New Abolition* by social ethicist Gary Dorrien, where he addresses the marginalization of black religion scholars as a matter of convention:

> The convention is that religious intellectuals no longer mattered by the end of the nineteenth century. In that case, black religious intellectuals did not matter whether or not they existed. Both verdicts got ballast from black academics of the early twentieth century that historians tend to favor—Ralph Bunche, Alain Locke, Abram Harris, E. Franklin Frazier, and Rayford Logan. All shared the customary academic prejudice against religion and religious intellectuals, contending that the black church was hopelessly provincial and conservative. So black social gospel intellectuals such as [Reverdy] Ransom, [Richard R.] Wright and [Mordecai] Johnson had no chance of being remembered, and even Thurman and Mays were overlooked for decades.[5]

All five of the black academics cited by Dorrien for being dismissive of religious intellectuals and the black church were professors at Howard University; three of the five are depicted in the 1950 "dream team" photo. He laments that historians have overlooked the contributions of Johnson, Thurman, and Mays as religious intellectuals. In his role as president, Johnson was responsible for bringing all of these academics to Howard, including the religion professors. Howard Thurman was the first to be appointed

4. Ta-Nehisi Coates, "Return of the Mecca?" Feb 19, 1999. http://www.washingtoncitypaper.com/news/article/13017139/return-of-the-mecca, accessed 23 December 2016.

5. Gary Dorrien, *The New Abolition: W. E. B. Du Bois and the Black Social Gospel* (New Haven: Yale University Press, 2015), 9.

dean of Rankin Chapel, serving from 1932 to 1944. During those years he established an international reputation in ecumenics, ethics, race relations, preaching and contemplative activism. Benjamin Elijah Mays was appointed dean of the School of Religion at Howard University from 1934 to 1940. He published two important studies of black religion in the 1930s, *The Negro's Church* with co-author Joseph Nicholson in 1933, and *The Negro's God* in 1938. Thurman moved on to become the first black dean of Marsh Chapel at Boston University, and Mays served with distinction as president of Morehouse College. Williams heartily acknowledges the impact both Thurman and Mays had at Howard and beyond as they gave voice to a "theology of race relations" in annual convocations that sought to address issues faced by black clergy and black churches in mainstream society. Moreover, they constructed a bridge of black religious thought "spanning from their day to the time of Howard black theologians such as J. Deotis Roberts, who, with his contemporaries, moved the discussion of black religion from merely challenging mainline white Christian church studies to advancing a self-defined black theology."[6] But it was Johnson's affinity for the social gospel that made Howard University a fertile ground for the development of a theory and theology of race relations during his tenure.[7] I would venture that this black social gospel became the signature organizing principle employed by Johnson to promote fulfillment of Howard's identity as The Capstone under his leadership.

What is significant about this view of the historic tension between public intellectuals at Howard University is that it discloses a fault line of critical disregard or rejection of faith-based approaches to addressing the disparities that African Americans experience. Yet, the black social gospel set forth at Howard by such luminaries as Johnson, Thurman and Mays was intentional in its acceptance of the scholarly contributions of others in the arts, sciences, humanities and the professions, notwithstanding the divisive politics that have strained relations between university administrators and faculty departments in general. Dorrien credits the Howard religion scholars as exemplars of a black social gospel that combined "black dignity and personhood with protest activism for racial justice, a comprehensive social justice agenda, an insistence that authentic Christian faith is incompatible with racial prejudice, an emphasis on the social ethical teaching of Jesus,

6. Williams, *Talented Tenth*, 162–63.
7. Williams, *Talented Tenth*, 42.

and an acceptance of modern scholarship and social consciousness."[8] In the case of the civil rights movement, religion goes "hand-in-hand" with local communities, activist organizing, and public intellectual discourse. I believe that at Howard we can affirm and implement Dorrien's call to "take the story back to the black social gospel tradition that pressed the issue of social justice, organized at the community and denominational levels, and created public intellectuals."[9]

The Capstone 1950 dream team not only signifies the marginalization of religion scholars, but also of women. For example, historian Merze Tate is conspicuously absent from the lineup, as is Dorothy Porter Wesley, author of *Early Negro Writing, 1760 to 1837* who fostered the global pre-eminence of Howard University's Moorland-Spingarn Research Center from 1930 to 1973. In the book, Coates offers a more or less even-handed acknowledgment of his encounters with his female professors in the classroom and the works of female writers in the library.

By his own testimony Coates invested more time in the library than in the classroom during his years as a student at The Capstone. However, his days in Moorland-Spingarn Research Center not only were well spent, but his story underscores the quality and impact of Howard's collection of African American scholarship across the disciplines. Coates vigorously embraced an aspect of Howard that many others miss, namely, that our Moorland-Spingarn Research Center is unparalleled internationally as a resource for students and scholars of matters pertaining to black lives. His narrative further establishes the significance of black subjectivity—in our library collections black people are prominent as authors and analysts, and not just as objects of scholarly investigation. Furthermore, Howard's collections support the research and writing of persons who are poised to perform serious engagement of the disparities black people face in the U.S. and globally. Our tools of intellectual engagement are operative in a broad range of academic disciplines: arts and sciences, engineering and architecture, business, communications, education, law, health sciences, social work, divinity, and the rest. Howard University is a vital repository of thought and research seeking justice, freedom and equality of opportunity for black people of all creeds, cultures, and nationalities.

8. Dorrien, *New Abolition,* 3.

9. Dorrien, *New Abolition,* 10.

CONCLUSION: CELEBRATION AND LAMENT

It seems clear to me that Coates did not write this book for the primary purpose of celebrating Howard University as The Mecca. Howard is important because of the avenues it offered to enable a bewildered kid from west Baltimore to acquire an authentically cosmopolitan adult identity and to achieve global acclaim as an award-winning journalist. Coates's experiences at Howard provided a frame of reference for him to lament the death of his friend Prince Jones, to process his son's tearful reaction to the news that the police officer who killed Michael Brown would not be held accountable, and to reconfigure his professional commitment to expose these disparities and injustices with his pen. As a Christian ethicist I am struck by the candor that fuels the eloquence of his prose, and especially by his refusal to mediate his expressions of grief and outrage with traditional appeals to faith and hope. I do not detect a whiff of dismissive contempt in Coates's own professions of atheism. On the contrary, I discern in the pages of *Between the World and Me* an earnest skepticism, an open heart and a keen intellect at the ready for critical engagement with issues that still press upon people of African descent at the midpoint of Howard's second century. His tone and temperament have motivated me to retrieve the ethical sensibilities of the black social gospel as a way forward for my colleagues and students who remain engaged in the vocation of theological scholarship and education, and to rediscover the antiquated moral compass embedded within this ethical tradition whose relevance and reliability bear urgently upon our present search for solutions that matter for black lives. So this conversation has helped me to refine and rename my own objective as a public intellectual, that is, to offer hope and equity as alternatives to dreams and plunder. I am deeply appreciative of the energizing moment Coates has captured in his work. In many ways he has inspired me to renew my resolve as a pilgrim of The Mecca and as a citizen of The Capstone.

3

BLACK FUTURES AND BLACK FATHERS

— Vincent Lloyd —

Ta-Nehisi Coates's memoir, *The Beautiful Struggle*, starts with a street fight.[1] The young Coates is in trouble, running from the violence of his Baltimore neighborhood. As Coates depicts it, the Black youth growing up with him inhabited a world of brutal chaos, stalked by violence inflicted by their peers and by police. Confronted acutely by this violence, fleeing from it, Coates reaches out to the only site of stability he can always count on. He calls his father. "When I was young," he writes, "my father was heroic to me, was all I knew of religion" (205).

Flash forward a quarter century. Coates himself is a father, raising a Black son. *Between the World and Me* is a meditation on American racism, but it is also, on its surface and at its core, a story of paternity.[2] The terms have changed in certain crucial ways, but the essential divinization of the paternal relationship has not. Coates describes his son as "God." While he represents his own father as distant, powerful, and wise, when Coates writes of his son he writes of the body. He describes incarnation: what is holy about his son (and himself) is located in the body.

1. Coates, *The Beautiful Struggle: A Memoir* (New York: Spiegel & Grau, 2008). Subsequent page references will be noted parenthetically in the text.
2. Coates, *Between the World and Me* (New York: Spiegel & Grau, 2015). Subsequent page references will be noted parenthetically in the text.

24

Coates is seemingly proud of his atheism, of the atheism in which he was raised by his father, but it is hard to miss the deeply theological resonances in Coates's two books. Coates does not believe in God, but he does believe in fathers—in a very strong sense, in the mystical power of paternity. Where Carl Schmitt described the theopolitical, background ideas about God giving shape to political ideas about sovereignty, we might see in Coates's writings the workings of the theopaternal.[3] Background ideas about God (shared cultural assumptions from a specifically Christian context) give rise to particular ideas about fatherhood. Indeed, Coates's repeated insistence on his atheism suggests just how strong a hold the traditional model of religiosity has for him, in contrast to the more diffuse language of spirituality that we might expect given the contemporary American religious landscape. Indeed, it may be the case that this traditional model of religiosity, of belief in an all-powerful being together with belief in an embodied God, does more than just shape how Coates depicts paternity. Coates's profusely, repeatedly denied belief in God may be displaced onto his views about fathers.

This is a problem. In the case of the theopolitical, complex theological debates in the background of political ideas about sovereignty are drastically simplified, giving rise to correspondingly simplistic political claims that are authorized by an aura of absolute truth, and those political ideas cannot be freely contested because the theological background on which they depend is always disclaimed. The result is the same for the theopaternal: the ideas about fatherhood at work are given their plausibility because of over-simplified theological claims, but there is no way to contest those theological claims because the theological register is ostensibly rejected. What results is not an intellectual problem about misunderstanding the concept of fatherhood. Rather, it is a problem that has to do with patriarchy and with racism, and particularly with how the two are entwined. The view of fatherhood implicitly supported by a simplistic theology is a key component of patriarchy (and with it heteronormativity), as it affirms the absolute power of the father and the privilege of the male heir; at the same time, this view of fatherhood affirms racial purity ensured by smooth transmission of racial status from father to son.[4]

3. This point is developed further in Lloyd, "From the Theopaternal to the Theopolitical: On Barack Obama" in Melanie Johnson-DeBaufre, Catherine Keller, and Elias Ortega-Aponte, eds., *Common Goods: Economy, Ecology, and Political Theology* (New York: Fordham University Press, 2015), 326–43.

4. For a recent exploration of these entanglements, see Grace Kyungwon Hong,

At its best, Africana thought contests this account of paternity.[5] In the work of James Baldwin, to take the key figure Coates attempts to emulate, Blacks do transmit values, knowledge, and wisdom from generation to generation, but this transmission is not identified with father to son transmission. Where Coates frames *Between the World and Me* as a letter to his son, Baldwin begins *The Fire Next Time* with a letter to his nephew. When Baldwin meditates on his own father, as he does brilliantly in "Notes of a Native Son" and his first novel, *Go Tell It on the Mountain*, his goal is to loosen the hold of authoritarian models of paternity. Indeed, Baldwin is quite explicit about how aesthetics (specifically, the practice of writing well) displaces authoritarian paternity, opening the possibility for inter-generational transmission that does not rely on semen and eggs. Instead, it relies on painting, poetry, song, and dance. In other words, Africana thought at its best severs the tie between biological reproduction and intergenerational transmission, in doing so opposing both patriarchy and white supremacy. In contrast, when Africana thought tries to follow white models, biological reproduction and intergenerational transmission are identified with each other: witness how Barack Obama's memoir is organized around his quest to find his biological father, which makes him capable of inhabiting his own manhood—and, eventually, the presidency.

Does re-envisioning paternity, when paternity is implicitly linked with theology, require re-envisioning God? Might a Black perspective on paternity open a pathway to understanding what it might mean to worship a Black God? This should not be such a radical suggestion. Aligning paternity with aesthetics rather than biology quite clearly improves the accuracy of the fatherhood metaphor for God. Biological reproduction is essentially worldly; aesthetics opens to that which is beyond the world, to beauty aligned with truth and goodness, all irreducible to worldly terms, all markers of participation in the divine. In other words, Black accounts of intergenerational transmission hold the possibility of righting our theology, in addition to combatting the idolatries of patriarchy and white supremacy, but this potential is quashed when such transmission is taken to be biological, when fathers are taken to be gods in the crude, authoritarian, heretical

Death beyond Disavowal: The Impossible Politics of Difference (Minneapolis: University of Minnesota Press, 2015).

5. Most famously, Hortense Spillers, "Mama's Baby, Papa's Maybe: An American Grammar Book," *Diacritics* 17:2 (1987), 65–81. See also Vincent Lloyd, *Religion of the Field Negro: On Black Secularism and Black Theology* (New York: Fordham University Press, 2018), chapter 5; on Baldwin in particular, chapter 2.

sense of the term. This is my worry about Coates's persistent emphasis on fatherhood.

It is also a worry about hope. The claim of this essay is that Coates's much-discussed pessimism is the only option available when fathers and gods are identified.[6] The only hope that would be possible is hope in worldly terms, that is, optimism, and Coates is right that optimism (about, for example, racial justice) is not warranted. He is wrong, however, that pessimism is the only alternative to optimism. There is also hope—hope made possible when secularism is rejected, when the world does not set the limits on our (theological, political, racial) imagination.

THE AUTHORITY OF THE FATHER

The first photograph of *Between the World and Me* depicts the author holding his infant son; the last photograph depicts the author wrapping his arm around his teenage son. Even before the opening scene of *The Beautiful Struggle,* the reader is confronted with biological reproduction positioned as the narrative's backbone through the opening illustration: a family tree. There is no doubt that these books are stories of paternity. In that vividly narrated opening scene in *The Beautiful Struggle,* Coates is fleeing and afraid, chased by neighborhood miscreants. "Son, I'm on the way" his father reassures (5). Like a superhero, his father arrives and saves the day: "Dad ran off into the swarming night," Coates writes. "For the first and only time, I was afraid for him" (7). After the rescue, the young Coates knew his father to be invincible. Whatever chaos or violence might surround the boy, the author, the father could withstand it. The father could bring order. (Note how, in contrast, Baldwin writes of the death of his father concurrent with the violent chaos of race riots.[7])

The power that Coates attributes to his father is both physical and intellectual. "He stood a solid six feet, was handsome, mostly serious, rarely angry" (12). His father was a man in charge of his emotions. He was deeply learned. Indeed, learning was his occupation: he was an archivist

---

6. See, for example, Melvin Rogers, "Between Pain and Despair: What Ta-Nehisi Coates is Missing," *Dissent,* July 31, 2015, https://www.dissentmagazine.org/online_articles/between-world-me-ta-nehisi-coates-review-despair-hope.

7. Baldwin, "Notes of a Native Son," In *Notes of a Native Son* (Boston: Beacon, 1955), 85–114. Coates's depictions of his father, including the physical descriptions and his holiness, follow Baldwin's essay very closely.

at Howard University, collecting and caring for great works of Africana thought. In other words, not only was this father omnipotent, he was also omniscient. If one wanted knowledge, the person to ask was Coates's father. And this role was sacred: Mecca is the name Coates gives to Howard, where his father worked compiling knowledge, and where Coates himself would eventually go to study. Coates's father continued his work at home, in the family's basement, called by his father a "temple," where he would collect, reprint, and sell books about Black life and thought (137). Like any sacred figure, Coates related to his father with "hatred and complete reverence" and describes how, despite knowing that his father was flawed, "he retained the aura of a prophet" (30).

Coates's father received his powers from another powerful man: Coates's grandfather. This grandfather, though also "intellectual," was religious, and attempted to transmit religious knowledge to his son; Coates's own father attempted to transmit Afrocentric knowledge to the young Coates, giving him esoteric books to read about the greatness of the Black race. These books took the place the Bible had held for Coates's grandfather, revered as the exclusive source of sacred knowledge. Indeed, Coates's father was militantly atheistic, and there was a ban on religious expression in the Coates household. When one of Coates's siblings was caught praying, his father responded, "You want to pray, pray to me. I put the food on this table" (20). This god-father even invented quasi-religious dietary rules for his family, prohibiting meat and restricting other foods. Coates describes his father's beliefs as "Consciousness," as "theology" that his father preached, or prophesied. All worldly things must be subordinated to Consciousness, even food and life itself, or so Coates understood his father to believe.

While Coates's father had extraordinary power, at least in his young son's eyes, this power did not usually extend beyond the household. In the streets and at school, brute force reigned. The closest that one could come to the authority of the father, on the streets, was to possess a gun. (That both father and gun stand for the phallus, for the cornerstone of patriarchy, requires no argument.) This was the path chosen by some of Coates's peers, but it was not his. For Coates, Africana knowledge was the only "sorcery to counter death for suede, leather, and gold" (107). In a world where premature death seemed likely if not inevitable, where there was no social or state authority that could be trusted to bring life stability, it was the sacred knowledge of his father that offered a chance at life, at new life instead of life en route to death.

Rather than power emanating from a position on top of the world, ruling over the world, on Coates's view his father's power came from his position among the marginalized. The powers that be in the world repressed truth; truth was only to be found in the shadows, among the oppressed, and many of the oppressed had themselves forgotten that they were bearers of truth. This was the source of Coates's father's intellectual power; his physical power similarly came about because of marginality. "My father swung with the power of an army of slaves in revolt. He swung like he was afraid, like the world was closing in and cornering him" (141). Because his efforts were continually stymied, Coates's father was filled with rage. This rage accumulated into physical power that was unleashed, by means of his belt, on his son.

What eventually allows the young, wayward Coates to become a man, to defy death, is finding his own entry point to that African wisdom of his father. Reading the countless books in the family "temple" may have primed him, but it was participation in an Afrocentric cultural organization that began to give his life meaning, on his account. That meaning coalesced only when the young Coates took up "traditional" African drumming. Like the guns that circulated around him but he rejected, the drum was another phallus; Coates is explicit about the connection. "The djembe, the way it hangs between the legs, is virility itself and has a special call to young boys looking for ways to express the change popping off inside. . . The drum sounded like a gun if guns were made to be music" (148). The boy experiences collective effervescence as he plays with his peers, against the background of repressed, esoteric Africana knowledge, and the boy becomes a man. Drumming offered access to the "pantheon of ancestors," connecting him with "the direct current to the Motherland" (150). (He also undergoes a "traditional" initiation rite.) His childhood had been lived in the shadow of his god-like father, but to come of age Coates needed to connect with the generations before, with the imagined African past that would allow him to wield his own masculinity in the present as he beat his drum.

THE BODY OF THE SON

In *The Beautiful Struggle*, Coates reports that his father has a dream: "mass resurrection" (14). This is Coates's theologization of a political aspiration. What revolution means, for his father, a former Black Panther, is a transformation of the masses. They would have new knowledge, a new self-understanding. They would realize that the history they have been taught in schools and throughout their lives by a system of white supremacy is wrong. They would realize the greatness of the African inheritance that was theirs. They would seize political power for themselves, and in this self-assertion they would have new life. Coates's father was very much aware of the temptations of the world and of the tendency of humans to desire what is not best for them. A transformation was needed, a conversion.

Coates's father had secularized his own father's Christian faith, and Coates further secularizes his father's account of conversion and resurrection. Yet the essential Christian background remains. Indeed, it becomes even more explicit in *Between the World and Me*. Coates's first book is a coming-of-age story where manhood is achieved by accessing the African ancestors and spirits guided by his god-like father, a process represented primarily as intellectual, as about belief, knowledge, and spiritual communion. Coates turns in his second book to the body. Resurrection is no longer connected to mental conversion; if it is possible, it now would mean resurrection of the body. This is announced from the very first page, from the very first line. It is Sunday morning, and Coates reflects on losing his body. The Sabbath timing is clearly significant, even if that significance is repressed. Even more significant is the occasion of this new reflection, this new book. It is a text addressed to Coates's son. Coates the father is reflecting, on Sunday, about possible bodily resurrection for Coates the son.

Coates's depiction of his own father had focused on distant power and intellectual authority, and Coates defended the possibility of god-like fatherhood for Black Americans, against the forces of white supremacy. In *Between the World and Me*, Coates defends the possibility of Christ-like sonship for Black Americans, the possibility that the absolute power and authority of a father could be transmitted to a child who is embodied. Just as the white world wanted to take knowledge away from the father, the white world wants to take the body away from the son. The challenge for the narrative of the more recent book is to show how incarnation might be possible, how knowledge of truth and bodily existence might coexist, despite the worldly forces aligned to prevent this possibility.

Paternity remains unequivocally good in *Between the World and Me*, as it was in Coates's first book. Coates now elaborates, arguing that race is the product of society, racist society, not the product of parentage. In other words, focusing on father to son transmission allows access to a relationship beyond race, and beyond worldly distortions more generally. The way racism works, concretely, is to capture the body of one who is marked as Black. "Racism is a visceral experience" (10). The body becomes vulnerable, the object of violence from the police but also from within the Black community itself as racial hostility deprives and distorts the Black community. In this chaos, with social norms distorted or absent, there is only brute force left—applied to the body. "To be black in the Baltimore of my youth was to be naked before the elements of the world," Coates writes (17). There was no place to turn for protection, no common authority to assure stability. While Coates describes this in the specific historical context of his youth in a drug- and violence-plagued Baltimore neighborhood, Coates also describes this as the existential meaning of Blackness. Coates's father was exposed to the elements, different elements, and so too will his son be exposed.

The Christomorphic tendencies in Coates's portrayal of his son are barely concealed. "You were the God I'd never had," he writes to his son (67). In contrast to his father, a distant and powerful god figure, his son is worldly, physically present, embodied. Whatever physical affection he may have desired but never received from his father he would lavish on his son. But incarnation is about more than embodiment. Coates's son fires up the author's own intellectual curiosity, waking his mind. Where Coates's father had taught him to understand himself in relation to (imagined African) tradition, his son teaches him to passionately pursue his own questions. Coates can become himself, can become an author, in response to such questions. These are questions about how the world fits together, why Blacks are marginalized, but most importantly, they are questions about the body. The profoundest questions of all, those prompted by Coates's child-god, are not questions about the meaning of justice or goodness or piety. They are questions about how a body that is so worldly, so subject to pain and violence, can exist together with a mind that seems above all such concerns. These are questions of our shared humanity, but they are posed particularly acutely by and for Blacks, whose bodies are especially vulnerable.

Coates's depiction of incarnation clearly depends on background assumptions about Christian theology, but because these assumptions are suppressed their over-simplicity goes unquestioned. On the one hand, the claim that Coates implicitly makes—that non-Blacks take their bodies for granted because of the illusion of invulnerability, while Blacks must face directly a profoundly human and ultimately irresolvable question about the body in its relationship to the mind (or something like it)—seems right.

The Christian story, similarly, calls attention to the fraught relationship between, on the one hand, bodily existence and vulnerability, and, on the other hand, absolute knowledge, truth, and power. The Christian theological tradition has struggled with the complexities of this problematic over two millennia. A hard separation between fallen body and God-given mind or spirit was long ago rejected as heretical; the natural world, including the body, is understood to be created good by God and so in some ways oriented toward God, even though many distortions interfere with that orientation. In short, by his insistence on his own atheism, Coates is cutting off access to precisely what he purports to desire: robust questioning of how we can relate to our vulnerable bodies.

According to Coates, the natural and apparently appropriate response to alienation from the body is affective investment in children. "Black people love their children with a kind of obsession"—a conclusion he describes as "a philosophy of the disembodied, of a people who control nothing, who can protect nothing" (82). Given the chaos and violence that characterize the world, and the lack of protection afforded to Blacks, the always-thwarted desire to protect one's own body is projected onto the child. Coates assures his son that he was loved by his parents, that he loved his parents, and that he loves his son—though he protests that this has nothing to do with "religious feeling" (88). Because of Black vulnerability, there is all the more investment in Black paternity. In one sense, this certainly is not a religious feeling: it is locating value—the only site of value in what Coates otherwise describes as a value-free universe—in worldly things, namely, fathers and sons. In another sense, this is a very religious claim. There are, in fact, many things that we value, and that Coates values; what he is really doing is locating the sites of absolute value, those that trump all other worldly values. He locates these in paternity. In a theological idiom, he embraces idolatry: treating certain worldly things (relationships with parents and children) as if they are God.

Oddly, despite the alienation of Blacks from their bodies that is the thesis of Coates's book, the bodies of Black women are understood outside of this context of alienation—at least from the perspective of the young Coates. When he went to the Mecca, Howard, he was impressed with the young women he encountered: "The physical beauty of the black body was all our beauty, historical and cultural, incarnate" (49). In contrast to Black men, for whom incarnation (joining the transcendental and the physical) is necessary but impossible, Coates sees no similar problem for Black women, even as he acknowledges the doubled vulnerability of the bodies of Black women. Here again deeper reflection on the theological would help untangle the knot into which Coates is weaving himself. If the body, as part of the natural world, is created good as well as beautiful, and if loving this beauty (regardless of gender) can orient us beyond the world, the beauty Coates witnesses among the Howard women need not be reduced to the (worldly) terms of libidinal desire that his prose invites.

If there is an obstacle to be overcome in the narrative of *Between the World and Me*, it is the obstacle elusively named in the title: that obstruction which prevents the protagonist-author from relating to the world like others—specifically, like whites. The book never directly names this obstacle, nor does it purport to show how it might be overcome. It is something like white supremacy, but Coates rightly avoids leaning on a label that could become a crutch, inhibiting deeper analysis. Rather than overcoming this obstacle, the book purports to show how Black Americans might live with it. Reading and writing, "study," are the tools for enduring white supremacy. This antidote starts even more basically, with asking questions. Questioning will not restore our bodies to ourselves, but asking, again and again, questions in dialogue with the thought of others, as we struggle to write, will make us aware of the loss of our bodies. When we are unaware of what, precisely, we are alienated from, we are deeply afraid. We know something is missing, and the inability to name the missing object terrifies. Questioning and studying help us name that object as the body.

On the one hand, questioning and study—that is, the book itself as an exemplary performance of these—are presented as the antidote to the fundamental problem posed in *Between the World and Me*. They quiet the terror of white supremacy as it manifests in bodily alienation. But Coates also presents another means of quieting that terror, and he does not attempt to reconcile the two. This other salve is paternity. He writes to his son, "I feel the fear most acutely whenever you leave me" (14). The book itself is an exemplary performance of questioning in a quite specific sense: it is questioning directed at future generations, directed from father to son. If only enough knowledge could be accumulated and transmitted to his son, in this public letter, then his son might live happily. Coates is repeating the ambition of his own father, with that "temple" of Africana esoterica in the family basement, transmitting wisdom from father (and father's fathers) to son. It turns out that the antagonist, that force inserting itself between Coates and the world, is really a displacement from that which inserts itself between Coates and his son. If only he could be the perfect father, transmitting himself wholly to his son, making his son into himself—then they could live without fear, in post-racial bliss (recall how Coates positions paternity outside of race).

HOPE AND OPTIMISM

Optimism is one of the targets of *Between the World and Me*. Coates labels it the Dream, and he labels optimists Dreamers. They believe that America is a land for all, blessed by God, moving steadily in the right direction, toward inclusivity, mutual respect, and all around happiness. But Coates does not distinguish between hope and optimism; he uses the concepts interchangeably, and interchangeably with the Dream.[8] Coates laments "all the people out there . . . reveling in a specious hope," by which he means the Dream, the belief that the nation is moving inevitably in the right direction (10).

Coates frames his ability to distance himself from the Dream, from normative American optimism, as a product of his atheist upbringing. Americans closely identify their nation with (the Judeo-Christian) God, he asserts, and with this conflation comes the sense of inevitable progress. Even though many Black Americans buy into the Dream, the marginalization of Blacks provides Blacks with the perspective necessary to demystify the Dream. "America understands itself as God's handiwork, but the black body is the clearest evidence that America is the work of men" (12). With this demystification, the myth of progress shatters; the nation is morally ambivalent, and it could become better or worse. Throughout the nation's history, many Americans have conducted themselves very badly, as has the nation as a whole. Coates's own view, growing out of his father's atheism, is decidedly less rosy than the Dream: "My understanding of the universe was physical, and its moral arc bent toward chaos then concluded in a box" (28). Coates the secularist sees no order in the universe beyond the physical world, sees the lower instincts of human beings, and concludes that the status quo (white supremacy) will persist or be exacerbated. In his youth, the streets of Coates's Baltimore neighborhood were chaotic; the only way to manage the violence was to form neighborhood gangs and to understand the gang codes that were enforced with violence. The nation, situated against the backdrop of chaos, is run by a white-supremacist gang with its

8. For an account of the distinction, see Christopher Lasch, *The True and Only Heaven: Progress and its Critics* (New York: Norton, 1991).

own codes, similarly enforced by violence. There is no reason to believe that racial justice is on the horizon.

But this is because Coates is a secularist—not just without religion but dogmatically excluding that which is beyond the "physical." In doing so, in his rejection of his grandfather's Christianity, he is replicating that piety, displaced onto paternity. In the face of worldly chaos, the only place to turn for comfort and security is the father and the son. The only hope in *Between the World and Me* is implicit: it is hope for the son, hope that the son will join in the revel of questioning and study. But this is a secularized theological hope. It is a hope for a future beyond the world, but it is, in its secularization, tied to the world—with the blood that joins father and son.

Coates declares, "The Dream is the enemy of all art" (50). This statement seems quite clearly true when the Dream is understood as optimism. If art at its best expresses imperfectly that which cannot be reduced to worldly terms, then allowing one's horizon to be set by worldly terms—the Dream—cripples artistic possibility. For Coates, the alternative to the Dream is nihilism: brief life in a physical, value-free world, then death.[9] But this does not bode well for art. All it can do is wallow in, or play with, the options on the table, endlessly repeating new configurations of what has already been done. Art loses its relationship to beauty, and thus to hope. Coates's own prose reflects this: he is a good stylist and a thoughtful writer, but his ideas are essentially those of others, reworked. He aspires to greatness, and his prose is often well-disciplined, but discipline alone is not enough to reach toward beauty. Coates is shackled to the world: in his first book, to his father; in his second, to his son.

This is the reason for Coates's pessimism. He presents it as a product of his atheism coupled with the fact of white supremacy, but actually it is a product of his displaced theology. The horizon of hope is limited by consanguinity, and against the background of white supremacy that leaves little room for Black hope. On the one hand, Coates is quite aware of the connection between paternity and divinity that he represents, and he is wary of it. He writes in *The Beautiful Struggle* that "fatherhood was dictatorship [and] its subjects were at the mercy of a tyrannical God" (206). But Coates's solution when he becomes a father himself is to act as a better father, a more

9. This is putting it in stronger terms than Coates himself would likely accept. My point—and I am certainly making it hyperbolically here—is about an orientation to the world. To what extent are we open to that which is orthogonal to the world entering into the world? If we are disposed to foreclose this possibility, it would limit our ability to appreciate and create beautiful work.

loving father. Switching from a wrathful god-father to a loving god-father does not address the more fundamental problem, namely, the identification of paternity and divinity. Coates substitutes love for hope and showers it on his son. He does not see this as motivated by hope for his son because he so thoroughly identifies with his son. It is they together against the morally vacuous world. They will question together, study together, be as human as they can be together, but the world will still be against them, as it is against all Black Americans.

What is lacking from Coates's narrative, because of his excessive focus on paternity, is a concern for sociality—and particularly for sociality as a site for hope.[10] As Coates freely admits, the excessive focus by Blacks on paternity is a product of white supremacy's foreclosure of the possibility of Black paternity. But why not embrace the other varied responses to this foreclosure? Why not embrace the aesthetic as an alternative mode of inter-generational transmission, or kinship structures that refuse the bounds of legality and heteronormativity? Again turning to theological resources cut off by Coates, why only imagine the body of Christ crucified two millennia ago as the model for sonship and not the body of Christ continually, glob-ally circulating in the Eucharist, or the body of Christ institutionalized in the church?[11] Why figure familial relations as only modeling those of Father or Son and not Spirit, as has so often and so creatively been done in Black religious communities?[12] Finally, instead of secularizing the resurrection into the birth of a biological son, why not appreciate the queer temporali-ties of Christian eschatology, creating openings for hope not circumscribed by the dimensions of the world?[13]

10. What about the apparent sociality found in Coates's account of, for example, the Howard University student community? It remains under the shadow of white suprema-cy, and (relatedly) it remains structured by patriarchy, as his descriptions of the gendered community norms suggest. Existing under the shadow of white domination, such spaces of apparent sociality, as described by Coates, are essentially reactive, mimicking and re-belling against the norms of white supremacy rather than opening to that which is wholly other. Thanks to Peter Dula for pressing me on this point.

11. See, for example, William Cavanaugh, *Torture and Eucharist: Theology, Politics, and the Body of Christ* (Oxford: Blackwell, 1998).

12. See, for example, Ashon Crawley, *Blackpentecostal Breath: The Aesthetics of Pos-sibility* (New York: Fordham University Press, 2017).

13. See, for example, Linn Tonstad, "Debt Time is Straight Time," *Political Theology* 17:5 (2016), 434–48.

4

SHALL WE AWAKE?

— JENNIFER HARVEY —

To awaken them is to reveal that they are an empire of humans and, like all empires of humans, are built on the destruction of the body.[1]

I do not know where you are sitting as you read this book. I do not know what the national, or even global, situation looks like. This is because of where I am sitting as I write. I sit today in a nation riveted. We are watching images of the Standing Rock Sioux and thousands who have come to join them. We are bearing witness to their courageous and defiant stand as water protectors, to their peaceful, prayerful, powerful resistance to the North Dakota Access Pipeline. We are reeling as state-sanctioned militarized violence descends on them daily and as images of terror fill our news feeds—images of peaceful, praying people covered in blood, horses shot down by law enforcement, and helicopters obscenely swirling overhead fill our news feeds.

1. Ta-Nehisi Coates, *Between the World and Me* (New York: Spiegel & Grau, 2015), 143.

Where I sit, it's been more than two years (August 2014) since the morning's news brought us reports that Ferguson, Missouri—a place most of us had never heard of—was on fire. Then, weeks of images filled our news feeds. These were all but indistinguishable from the iconic images that came out of Selma in 1965 or Detroit in 1967 and are now seared into our national memory; of protests, riot-geared police, and young people fleeing tear-gas. Then came Baltimore in spring 2015. That summer nine African-American Christians were massacred during Bible study and a national discussion ensued over the Confederate flag. In summer 2016 two Black men were killed as videotape rolled, communities across the nation erupted again in outraged protest, and a sniper killed seven police officers at a massive, peaceful rally in Dallas. Fall brought yet more footage of police killing unarmed Black people—we saw Terence Crutcher's killing in Tulsa and heard audio of Keith Lamont's now-widow cry—"Don't shoot him! He has no weapon!" followed by sounds of a fuselage of bullets. This time the images of protest, riot gear and tear gas flowed out of Charlotte, North Carolina.

I am sitting in a nation in racial crisis, the outcome of which will be uncertain for some time. In this context, it's appropriate to wonder if we may be experiencing the tremors of an awakening from "the Dream" about which Ta-Nehisi Coates writes in *Between the World and Me*. Coates evokes, describes and paints into view, in ways that rend the soul, a nightmare-masked-as-dream.

From where I sit the Dream seems unlikely to hold. The clash of history with the present is creating tremors that may bring an end to this nightmare-of-a-dream. Perhaps a seizure of violence means we dare hope for a liberating wakefulness. But it's hard to know, and I am afraid of violence. Still, as I let Coates's work rend my soul I welcome the tremors, even through my fears, because of what Coates brings into view: a reality more ultimate than the one we can experience while asleep. And a search for connection with ultimacy is, of course, the very essence of the "religious."

It's sitting amidst tremors, then, that I want to explore the ways Coates's *Between the World and Me* coheres with the work of Willie Jennings who also evokes, describes, and paints this reality into view. Jennings insists we see our diseased theological imagination, and while he writes within and committed to religion, a world in regard to which Coates remains publicly on the outside, the cohesive probing of race and religion in the writing of these two enables a deep vision of where we actually are as a nation. As an ethicist engaged with religion—both in study, but also as the venue and scaffolding for my own activist commitments and resistance—I find this vision to be life-giving even as it shakes me to my core. For it opens critical insights into the "now what," which is the question about which I am ultimately concerned.

THE TERROR OF A DISEASED IMAGINATION

Every time I teach my Race, Religion and Civic Culture class students struggle to contend with the ways Christianity was of a piece with the mechanisms of genocide and displacement of Native peoples and the plundering dislocation and enslavement of African peoples on this land-base that became the United States. They find the history devastating and experience overwhelming moral contradictions. They yearn for a resolution of these contradictions that will allow them to condemn in clear terms white-Euro, colonial-settler violence, while remaining hopeful about the tradition of Christianity.

My students inevitably offer a few stock explanations as they attempt to move through the intellectual and spiritual dislocation our studies compel. "Well, obviously those people weren't *real* Christians," they say. "These people totally misunderstood that Christianity is *actually* about love." "Anyone who used arguments from the Bible to justify what they did to Native or African peoples were just *using* Christianity to do what they really wanted to do."

With good reason they find some justification for these explanations when we study the diverse expressions, beliefs and practices of Black Christianity, or the ways forms of Native Christian practice manifested as resistance to the white, colonial-settler project. Nonetheless, their relief as they run toward such supremacy-resistant forms of Christianity for answers gives away the extent of their thirst. They are ready to consume any explanation that might allow them the relief of standing back, removed and viewing from afar just what went wrong. But the reality is more difficult. Even supremacy-resistant religious practices do not resolve the fundamental, epistemic shift compelled if we take race and white, colonial-settler supremacy seriously.

A number of things are striking about my students' reactions. One is their presumption that a pure, true, original form of Christianity even exists; as if a religious tradition can somehow be separate from people and untarnished by the humans who practice and claim it. I believe no such thing. Religion cannot exist outside of the diverse communities that embody it in messy, complex and sometimes incoherent ways.

More salient is that my students' reactions belie a resistance that goes beyond the intellectual difficulty of comprehension, and is evidence of great pain. I see a heartfelt longing for redemption. Especially (though not only) true for those who identify as Christian and especially (though not only) true for students who are white, there is something about the gravity of the loss that comes when recognizing a Christianity so implicated in racial and colonial-settler violence that is almost too much. Something deep about who and what "we" are seems to be on the line

I have always refused to allow my students the relief they seek through simplistic explanations or quick moves to distance themselves. But, I have struggled to understand why even my refusals never seem to get to the heart of things. My refusals themselves sound simplistic and never seem to adequately articulate the dense weight of our collective, shared global inheritance.

When I encountered Willie James Jennings's, *The Christian Imagination: Theology and the Origins of Race* a few years ago I began to understand why this was the case. It's worth emphasizing that this understanding is still new, emerging, and underdeveloped for me. Jennings's book is game-changing and epic-shifting. I am still wrestling with what Jennings's text, like Coates's, insists we see and understand, and I will be for some time to come. Both Jennings and Coates are difficult—in emotional and spiritual terms as much as intellectual ones.

The Christian Imagination goes well beyond exploring how Christianity was deployed and implicated in the so-called era of discovery—appropriately entitled the era of European conquest, genocide, and displacement. Jennings uses the discursive utterances of figures who were key in the large-scale work of commodifying peoples and places in this misnamed "era of discovery" to provide a devastating genealogy of the violence and, ultimately, epistemic distortion of our most formative theological imaginaries.

The commodification of peoples and lands was enabled by and enabled, was produced by and produced, racialization. The imperial process of conquest and displacement was thick, and the material and discursive dimensions of this process were of a piece. For Jennings this entire era literally marks an existential and physical cleavage between what existed before and everything that has come since. It is only from the "since" and, thus, from within the diseased theological imagination this era produced that we envision, experience and (mis)understand ourselves today, move physically through the world, and contend with matters of human relations and the fractures that race and colonial-settlers' identities and realities insert into these relations.

Jennings's project is akin to describing to a goldfish, who has only ever known life in the water, the feel, nature and significance of the fishbowl. This is what makes his work so hard to read and harder to talk about. Jennings is not describing Christians misusing theology or doctrine to justify bad things (both of which are versions of my students' explanations for Euro-white Christian involvement in slavery and genocide). He is not even talking about race being constructed through a misguided attempt to implement or justify what Europeans Christians were up to.

Jennings is bringing into view a dense co-production of everything. This includes, fundamentally, a new theological anthropology. Earth and place, which, prior, had been intrinsically constitutive of how human identity was conceptualized and experienced, became disarticulated from each other conceptually and experientially even while they were physically (and violently) wrenched apart in material reality. In this forcible separation from place, everything became caught and contained—quite literally—within an emerging racialization of reality and existence. In a sense, human identity, which prior, had been conceived and/or experienced as en-placed, was re-Created. This creation was a "theological" act. More devastatingly, re-Creation manifested through the realization of a racial scale, which made whiteness the (divine) supreme Creator in a very real sense.

In an early part of this work Jennings offers just one of countless glimpses of what he gestures toward in this work when he describes an early moment in the imperial, colonial project.

> Europeans enacted racial agency as a theologically articulated way of understanding their bodies in relation to new spaces and new peoples and to their new power over those spaces and peoples. Before this agency would yield "the idea of race," . . . or even a fully formed "racial optic" on the world, it was a theological form—an inverted, distorted vision of creation that reduced theological anthropology to commodified bodies.[2]

2. Willie James Jennings, *The Christian Imagination: Theology and the Origins of Race* (New Haven & London: Yale University Press, 2010), 58.

This entire theological production transpires through the concrete flesh-and-blood activity and material reconfiguration of relations—relations between peoples, land and place, and among "diverse" peoples, who now get placed into a "race."

The reconfiguration that accomplished and generated this production is still operative today. It is the genealogical root of the images flowing in from Standing Rock and of the experiences of Black U.S.-Americans whose bodies are made targets by the bullets of the state. But it is more than this. It's also the episteme now within which life operates: the "how" we see everything and "how" we see of everything. It is a diseased imagination from within which all things are perceived and through which we live all things—including our lives religious.

The displacement that was both product of an emerging *racial* identity and the imposition of racial identity on others eventually created "race" as a shallow, paltry container for identity. Jennings writes, "Without place as the articulator of identity, human skin was asked to fly solo and speak for itself."[3] And when we observe Native peoples being assaulted by militarized violence as they stand praying in a place, the inadequacy of so much of how we talk about "race" is so very evident even as we see legacies of Christian colonial-settler participation indicted.

Given the inadequacy of words for capturing our own seeing or bringing an episteme into view (the fishbowl), it cannot be overstated the degree to which Jennings gets at the deepest, most intimate, moral and spiritual notions of existence and the essential distortions within which we live. The theological imagination is diseased in ways we almost cannot recognize. As Jennings puts it, "It will not be easy to articulate the material reality of displacement because it is articulation of a loss from within the loss itself."[4] The era of discovery not only changed the globe and the condition of peoples throughout the globe, it re-created the most meta-level, epistemic view and conceptual experience of worlds and people. There simply is no "outside" of this process, which was and is simultaneously material, racial, and religious (Christian).

A myriad of theological postures and frameworks were articulated throughout this era. To offer just a few of Jennings's examples: the apologetic of "hidden treasures," which described global resources as placed there by God so Europeans would venture out and find them, thus making

3. Jennings, *Christian Imagination,* 64.
4. Jennings, *Christian Imagination,* 37.

conquest not merely justifiable but indicative of the desires and designs of God's heart; missionary debates over whether enculturation of African peoples could be "legitimately" separated from work to evangelize Africans further ensconced African peoples in a Euro-western episteme of universalism (as in, the divine can be found "there too"); whiteness not only as Creator of but as an optic that imposed spatial (as in, chronological) differences among peoples who existed in history *at the same time* (those deemed "primitive" as ancient and the "civilized" as modern even as they existed/exist in a concurrent moment); whiteness as simultaneously a way of seeing even as the activity of such seeing actualized the "seers."[5]

In wrestling with the density of this theological production the reason my responses to my students seem inadequate becomes clear. Even if I can articulate that we cannot separate religion from the behaviors of peoples who embody it, the entirety of our classroom conversation, study, and inquiry is unfolding already inside the fishbowl. While our dialogue occasionally gives way to a peripheral, momentary glimmer of the fishbowl, the size, significance, and encompassing power of the container mean that it slips from view nearly as quickly as we gesture toward it.

Bodies and land. Both displaced. Both commodified. All contained within the ocular gaze of the hierarchical racial scale of whiteness, performed and constituted as and through theological vision and action/being. "Centrally, I register the effects of the reconfiguration of bodies and space as a theological operation," writes Jennings.[6]

Race became the new ground replacing land and places as "signifiers of identity,"[7] and this becoming was and remains theological. No wonder, says Jennings, that a tradition that originates in response to a claim about the most profound intimacy possible—namely, the divine becoming enfleshed in embodiment—came to yield communities of diverse "racial" identities who were and remain so unknown to and distant from one another. The diseased theological imagination through which Christianity is now lived and experienced rended them/us apart and separate in space (time), place, and identity. And it is the fractured nature of those relationships that are being powerfully called into question in the tremors of this moment.

5. Jennings, *Christian Imagination*, 59.

6. Jennings, *Christian Imagination*, 24.

7. Jennings, *Christian Imagination*, 60.

THE TERROR OF "THE DREAM"

I read Coates on race only having already had the epistemic contours of my understanding of Christianity's complicity in the European, colonial-settler project ruptured—my framework turned inside-out in ways I will never be able to turn inside-in again. My first reading of *Between the World and Me* left me transfixed with Coates's brilliance and the sheer beauty and power of his writing.

Among the many things Coates has to say, among the most powerful has to do with the sheer, ravaging plunder of Black life as the very basis and essence of white U.S. nationhood and identity. In all of his writing, Coates makes clear that the racialized violence and racialized economic plunder on which this nation is built is fundamentally constitutive of white U.S.-American identity.

As with the phenomenon in regard to which Jennings is giving vision and voice, the constitutive process Coates brings into view too is a process more dense than one accurately understood as "good" people doing very "bad" things. That kind of process is easily reversed or at least challenged with good arguments, better persuasion or more effective moral checks and balances. Not so the Dream. The Dream is nothing less than false existence itself. The Dream is a state of being caught; entombed inside the false existence of whiteness. It's a state of being that is produced through an entangling dance of violence and plunder that is choreographed through rhetorical, visual and ideological discourses of identity, supremacy, inferiority and fear.

It's at the point of the Dream that Coates's work coheres so deeply with Jennings's. For what Coates reveals is that it's not merely because the material seductions of racism are so powerful that white Americans are loathe to wake ourselves from the Dream. Nor is it merely that we have consumed, inhaled, and injected so many lies and myths—and with such ritualized repetition—that waking from this nightmare-so-pleasurable would never occur to us. Each of these may be the case. But the crisis here is that any or all attempts to see our actual racial condition in the U.S. is already mediated through or take place from within a state of slumber that is posturing as wakefulness (the movie *Inception* comes to mind). This is especially true for white U.S.-Americans.

How does one even find ground from which to consider the possibility of or means for waking from a state of slumber when the most salient characteristic of that slumber is its ability to cause the sleeper to presume they are already awake? Even if we were not emotionally, politically, spiritually, intellectually invested in sustaining this nightmare-so-pleasurable (and we are these things), even if every ounce of our being utterly desired a state of wakefulness (and we do not), the journey to waking (the "how") is evasive.

It's worth noting that the same seductions, creations and re-creations that transpired through the so-called era of discovery were of a piece with the processes that led to the establishment of the U.S.-American project in a political and material sense. It's worth noting that the same existential trappings and episteme within which we are all caught as a result of the so-called era of discovery is the same false meta-reality out of which the identity "U.S.-American" exists in an ideological and existential sense. Coates does something very different with religion than Jennings does and would be unlikely to find the word "theological" useful. But even as the discourse and nomenclatures of these two writers are distinct, what they expose for us to see are parts of the same deep, inextricable tangle of physical activity and material realities with the densely intellectual, spiritual, emotional, and rhetorical movements that create our existential and epistemological trappings. A diseased theological imagination and a terrorizing Dream both constitute the world.

To that end, *Between the World and Me* begins with the epistemic awareness that those of us caught in the Dream are not anything other than embroiled as flesh and blood in racial violence, injustice and plunder of darker-skinned bodies. The challenge and crisis of white U.S.-America is this: *we are what we are.* We are the very horrors through which this nation-state came into existence politically and carved out an identity existentially; we are the trajectory to which we (so far) seem mostly willing to re-commit in our slumbering state.

This is what we must understand about the news cycles in regard to which, from where I sit, we stand riveted. The abuses of Black and brown bodies simply are not—not ever—the act of rogue individuals or the unjust. They are not places where our basic identity as nation or our principles have gone awry. Instead, Coates writes for example, they are "the product of the democratic will" (79). In the discourse about police violence that has transpired since long before August 2014, for example, we can never talk about a few bad apples. Coates dismisses talk of sensitivity training and body cameras because "The truth is that the police reflect America in all of its will and fear." Talk of cameras and sensitivity trainings simply allow those caught in the Dream "to pretend that there is a distance between their own attitudes and those of the ones appointed to protect them" (78).

In his writing as a journalist Coates's corpus traces the historical details, the legal decision-making, the fraud, the specific acts by specific people, states and institutions in order to provide a detailed account of precisely how the plunder has been accomplished. The entire operation has been accomplished within the normative workings of the Declaration of Independence, the Constitution and so much "law and order" in the United States.

In "The Case for Reparations," Coates traces in devastating detail the life story of Clyde Ross. Ross and his family's experiences are contextualized within the larger historical movements of African-American life amidst changing racial eras in the nation—in each era death-dealing, anti-Black violence and systemic, institutional and personal fraud and dispossession remain constants.[8] Similarly with his work on mass incarceration, Coates details the devastating impact the prison industry—and the mechanisms by which it comes to be—has had on Black families. He traces the "business-as-usual" function of prisons in the larger work of a nation-state built on plunder of Black bodies, families, communities.[9]

There is never any danger that Coates will leave unturned or unmarked in his work the "how," the "who" and the "where." The nature, cost, and perpetration of the plunder are splayed out for all of us to see. By the time his documentation is complete the connective tissue between the existence of the Dream and the material mechanisms that produce and sustain it is thoroughly mapped. Like Jennings's emphasis on the materiality of the displacement, which has spawned a distorted, diseased imaginary, the inner-workings and bloody underbelly on which the Dream depends is rendered clear in Coates's journalism. Moreover, the moral passivity (an understatement) required to tolerate such a state makes it beyond argument that the white among us really are in a state of deep slumber.

Whether or not we who are white can wake up is another question altogether. Nor is it Coates's question or concern. Indeed, he instructs his son—to whom *Between the World and Me* is written—directly that it is also not to be his question, "I do not believe that we can stop them, Samori,

8. Ta-Nehisi Coates, "The Case for Reparations," in *The Atlantic*, June 2014, http://www.theatlantic.com/magazine/archive/2014/06/the-case-for-reparations/361631/.

9. Ta-Nehisi Coates, "The Black Family in the Age of Mass Incarceration," in *The Atlantic*, October 2015, http://www.theatlantic.com/magazine/archive/2015/10/the-black-family-in-the-age-of-mass-incarceration/403246/.

because they must ultimately stop themselves" (151). *Between the World and Me* is Coates's articulation of his journey to find a way to live. He explains to his son, "the question of how one should live within a black body, within a country lost in the Dream, is the question of my life." He also writes, "Constant interrogation has freed me from the terror of disembodiment" (13).

Coates is not writing for white U.S.-Americans, and it's important I explicitly state my understanding of that fact. (Indeed, Coates has evaded more than once the question of why white folks are so taken with his work, given that he is not writing for us. In response to that question in one interview, he says, "The history is what it is. And it is disrespectful, to white people, to soften the history."[10] There's something telling in this response about the power of rare truth-telling experienced even among those who slumber.) It's important, because even as I honor that the question about white wakefulness from slumber is not Coates's question, it is my question.

In the closing section of this essay I want to engage the urgency of white colonial-settler waking as a religious question. In an attempt to respond to Jennings's work with the gravity his genealogy demands, I want to consider the notion of religion as the practice of waking up and make the counterintuitive move (given Coates's rejection of religion) to suggest that Coates's work enables a vision of how this can be pursued, the only way this could be pursued, even from within a theological imagination that is diseased.

Jennings's and Coates's work together compel recognition of an embodied set of practices necessary for *religious* response to the awareness of disease, plunder, and slumber. The possibility of embodied practice—aimed at waking up—also turns me back toward the urgency of the "now what?" that, again, is always the question with which I remain ultimately concerned.

RELIGION AS THE PRACTICE OF WAKING UP

Who and what "we" are is on the line. Standing riveted before images of the Standing Rock Sioux water protectors, the righteous anger of fires and courageous protest coalescing in Black communities across the nation, and

10. Felice León, "Ta-Nehisi Coates on Why Whites Like His Writing," October 25, 2015, http://www.thedailybeast.com/articles/2015/10/25/why-do-white-people-love-ta-nehisi-coates-work.html.

the riot gear, tear gas, assault weapons, and helicopters that rise to encounter and confront these resistance movements have everything to do with religion. The fractures in our human relationships, of which these tremors are so indicative, cannot be ignored by those who are engaged with religion—whether through study, in activist commitments, or both. Indeed, if by religious we mean orientation to ultimate reality, and if in Coates and Jennings we catch a glimpse of the false existence within which we are caught—a state removed from connection with ultimacy—then these tremors, because they portend awakening, are, at core, religious.

Before going further, a word about Coates's take on religion is needed. At one level, Jennings's genealogy goes a long way to make Coates's well-known rejection of religion understandable. This rejection might be read in terms of the overt participation of Christianity and white Christians in the terrors of the Dream. In one of many places in which Coates writes of the hard choices he has made about how and what to his teach his son he writes: "I knew that I must trouble you, and this meant taking you into rooms where people would insult your intelligence . . . and disguise their burning and looting as Christian charity. But robbery is what this is, what it always was" (101). If we're talking about white Christianity and white U.S.-American religiosity, then, both of which permeate the U.S.-American project, it's no surprise Coates would have no use for such a tradition.

At another level, however, Coates's rejection goes much deeper than merely a clear-eyed recognition of white Christian participation (then and now) in plunder. Coates's rejection is lodged in terms of existential-level understandings and interpretations of the meaning of and claims about ultimacy and divine agency. Coates is not anti-Christian. Coates is an atheist. Whatever the totality of his reasoning for atheism, those he lets his readers in on are compelling. He writes to his son, "You must resist the common urge toward the comforting narrative of divine law, toward fairy tales that imply some irrepressible justice. . . ." Instead, invoking what he has previously described as the meaning of life, he writes "Perhaps struggle is all we have because the god of history is an atheist and nothing about his world is meant to be . . ." (70).

Any serious engagement with global and U.S.-American history as it comes through the experience of Native and African peoples can only arrive at such a conclusion. This world was most certainly not meant be. Any assessment concluding otherwise reiterates an understanding of matters that has already succumbed to the diseased imaginary produced by these same atrocities. Bearing witness to the "god of history" in a world such as this is, indeed, a call to bear witness to an atheist god; to do otherwise is to career towards apology for genocide and plunder.

Yet, it is important at this juncture to name the reality that the religion Coates rejects—at least as he writes of it in *Between the World and Me*—is a particular type and presumes a specific conception of the divine. The notion of god here is one that emerges, at least partially, from traditions best described as escapist. That is, traditions in which god is conceived as solution to unending crisis, a "go to" as an explanation of the incomprehensible or a being in regard to which questions of theodicy are resolved too easily. This is a very limited understanding of "the religious."

I have no investment in writing against Coates's atheism. But, scholarly and political responsibility compel me to bring into view the ethically and spiritually challenging complexities womanist scholarship and religious thought bring to the same realities about which Coates writes. Womanist religious thought engages such realities without recourse to any of the too-easily-resolved answers Coates charges "religion" with presenting.

Eboni Marshall Turman, for example, challenges the way even Black religious thought has elevated an emphasis on the broken body—valorizing brokenness in a manner that enables the breaking of Black women's bodies and misogyny in the Black church. She writes toward a theology oriented around the profundity of divine embodiment in the flesh, Black flesh in particular.[11] In Turman I hear echoes of the love of flesh and journey-through-struggle that comes through as well in Coates's work. I hear in Turman a radical epistemological intervention. Hers is intent on re-knitting and re-doing that which was rended in the so-called era of discovery and the disease it unleashed.

Emilie M. Townes writes about searching for paradise in a world full of the deadly allure of theme parks.[12] Townes calls the religious to the activity of lament as the only way to articulate, see and know truthfulness.[13] I hear in Townes an insistence on making plain all of the plunder and violence. For, she marks lament as the only route through which we might journey, however slowly and in struggle, out of nightmares-masking-as-dream and

---

11. Eboni Marshall Turman, *Toward a Womanist Ethic of Incarnation: Black Bodies, Black Church and the Council of Chalcedon* (New York: Palgrave Macmillan, 2013).

12. Emilie M. Townes, *Breaking the Fine Rain of Death: African American Health Issues and a Womanist Ethic of Care* (1998; repr., Eugene, OR: Wipf & Stock, 2006), 168–86.

13. Townes, *Breaking the Fine Rain of Death*, 9–25.

toward wholeness and hope. This is not at all far removed from that toward which Coates calls.

Again, I emphasize these diversities in religious tradition—particularly Black religious traditions—not out of any interest in persuading Coates to embrace religion or god, nor to hold him responsible for making visible a more complicated understanding of religious thought and practice. But, I do want to write against the erasure of profoundly complex conceptions, experiences and theologizing of Christian religious traditions that in fact resonate deeply with the kind of "meaning seeking" about which Coates is passionate. These existing wisdoms and witnesses are not visible in Coates's description of religion or ultimacy, and they deserve to be seen.

More to the focus of this chapter, it is the fact of the complexity of the "religious" that entices me into seeing the religious at work in *Between the World and Me* and compels me to risk using language Coates would not embrace to talk about his work. This as a way to find routes toward the "now what?" from a place of being appropriately stunned to near silence and despair given the encompassing reality of a diseased imaginary and the power of slumber, yet to experience a yearning for a way through nonetheless.

To that end, there are three dimensions of Coates read in light of Jennings that invite re-visualization and re-orientation toward a religious "now what" in this moment. All speak to the urgent query about human relationships fractured and destroyed, made distant and alien, in the context of white, colonial-settler supremacy. Indeed, Coates's work enables response to the despair that a glimpse of the diseased theological imagination engenders and enables glimpses of viable routes through to awakening; the only hope of meaningful living in a world full of tremors.

It's in Coates's articulation of the meaning of his own journey that the first of these religious responses emerges. Early in *Between the World and Me* Coates describes what he learned from the "old heads" that taught him to be "politically conscious." This political consciousness, he writes, is "as much a series of actions as a state of being, a constant questioning, questioning as ritual, questioning as exploration rather than a search for certainty" (34). I suggest that Jennings's and Coates's assessment of our condition could compel us to relentlessly question our political context as a requisite form, ritual, and posture.

Rather than answers or improved theological positions, doctrines or rationales, relentless questioning as religious practice is the only posture that demonstrates responsive reverence for the sacred reality revealed in the genealogy Jennings lays bare. There are no answers we can construct as we sit within a diseased imagination. There are only postures we might take in the hope of finding new routes through. To return to my students and my classroom, let us acknowledge we are caught within an optic, episteme, fishbowl, Dream, false existence—however we try to give language to our condition—from within which viable paths through are not only virtually impossible to bring into view, but which are also envisioned by diseased seeing and seers. Relentless questioning as ritual, therefore, is not only the only way to embody our desire for contact with ultimacy, it is the only hope of moving toward such, however liminal and fleeting it may always remain.

Only questioning can lead to the possibility—however remote it may be—of an awakening and the awakening it might engender is appropriately understood as a religious one. In the wake of Jennings's paradigm-shifting text there are, for those of us who seek to be "religious," no answers. There can only be relentless questions. This is a ritual posture to which we are compelled in light of this work.

This insight relates quite directly to a second religious offering in Coates's work. This emerges out of the meaning-making and life-giving experience to which Coates testifies as he names his commitment to struggle. Writing from within and through living in a nation of people caught in the Dream, Coates tells his son that "struggle" is the only thing that is "under your control" (107). This regardless of whether the outcome is secure. "History is not solely in our hands," Coates writes, "And still you are called to struggle, not because it assures you victory but because it assures you an honorable and sane life" (97).

In the same vein Coates, an atheist, dares to write of the "meaning of life," and "rapture." On the experience of the meaning of life he recounts the impact on himself, as a father, of knowing the vulnerability of his Black son and of the fear that comes with such recognition. But he goes on to say:

> I am sorry that I cannot make it okay. I am sorry that I cannot save you—but not that sorry. Part of me thinks that your very vulnerability brings you closer to the meaning of life, just as for others, the quest to believe oneself white divides them from it. (107)

The latter part of this statement is particularly revelatory. If one leaves an encounter with these two writers convinced that whiteness and the cleavage of the so-called era of discovery have left white U.S.-Americans ensconced in the Dream and trapped in diseased imaginaries, a commitment to struggle is all that remains for those who want to wake. Yet here too something essentially orientating toward ultimacy transpires in such a commitment.

The contours of struggle are certainly not the same for white U.S.-Americans as they are for Black Americans and for Native peoples. I am working hard to not inappropriately use Coates's words. Coates, for example, in the passage above, names his own son's vulnerability as putting him closer to the meaning of life and in so doing names the difference in subjectivity, embodiment and types of struggle that may be life-giving among people of different races. White colonial-settler peoples do not come with the same vulnerabilities, even if our lives too are finally on the line.

Nonetheless, if the relentless quest to question is the religious posture necessary to awakening, and if it is awakening that holds the possibility of life, meaning, connection with that which is ultimate, it is clear from Coates's testimony that struggle is the essence of a religious practice. Coates has laid out the terms of a search for "paradise in a world full of theme parks."[14] And his quest for truth and commitment to struggle, he writes, have "awarded me a rapture that comes only when you can no longer be lied to, when you have rejected the Dream" (116). The terms are different when one lives not only as one among those who have been lied to but as one who has done more of the lying. Yet the rejection of the Dream, the relentless question and struggle to reject the Dream, is no less a religious quest for the white, colonial-settler, U.S.-American person than it is the condition for the possibility of rapture for a Black atheist writer.

Third, but most importantly, we who are caught in the Dream cannot ultimately think our way outside of a diseased theological imagination; nor can we who are caught in slumber create ideas that are powerful or re-formed enough to successfully wake ourselves up. The ultimate response to the question "now what?" comes out of Jennings's and Coates's ability to lay out in plain view the genealogies from whence the terror and disease comes.

Awakening means seeing ourselves revealed as participants in the creation of empire built on the destruction of bodies.[15] The diseased imaginary and the Dream came through action, violence, plunder. Thus the only way through to a re-formation is also a path of action—material response, the

14. Townes, *Breaking the Fine Rain of Death*, 168.

15. Emilie M. Townes, *Womanist Ethics and the Cultural Production of Evil* (New York: Palgrave Macmillan, 2006), 97–107.

birthing of a different imaginary through movement of bodies and mobilizing reparation. This movement must be responsive to the very same conditions and atrocities that generated the disease and the very tremors that are now portending a mass awakening. This is a flesh-and-blood embodiment of theology in a world caught in a nightmare-dream.

If the material struggles over the water in North Dakota and the killings of Black people are the tremors revealing a more ultimate reality constituting the actual "what" of our lives, only through activity that addresses, redresses, challenges, mobilizes, changes and postures in a seeking-to-be-in-solidarity can the possibility of re-shaping and re-forging the theological, moral and political imagination come into view. Only moving our bodies in postures of relentless questioning and struggle enables the possibility that those caught within a white colonial-settler Dream can awaken.

From where I sit, decisive action and activism in support of and responsive solidarity to the resistance movements unfurling across this land, is religious activity. It is the religious activity necessary, the essence of the search for ultimate reality, on the part of those who dare ask "now what?" after standing riveted with images and taking seriously a work like Jennings's or Coates's. For diseased moral, political, theological imaginaries may only be treated, healed, and transformed through action, and these actions must be engaged at the very same material location where the plunder transpired. That is the religious call I hear in Coates.

I don't know what kind of world you are sitting in as you read this book. I only know that from where I am sitting, embodied motion and movement is religious activity. Today it is the essence of religion: religion is and must become the living practice of waking up.

5

THE AMERICAN NIGHTMARE
AND THE GOSPEL OF PLUNDER

— David Evans —

For Negroes that dream contained a strong dose of such stuff as
nightmares are made of.[1]

I was the lone Black student, fulfilling one of my final graduation re-
quirements, among approximately twenty white students enrolled in a
Christian college cross-cultural program on the south side of Chicago during the summer of 1999. Graduating from a Christian college was a dream
for me and, as a first-generation college student, it was my family's dream
as well. I was positioning myself to live the American Dream. However,
that summer I experienced two events that would significantly shift my
relationship to that Dream. On Friday June 4, I received news that my first
son was born. The wondrous reality that I had become a father quickly

---

1. Ralph Ellison, *Shadow and Act* (New York: Vintage International, 1995), 304.

turned to fear for his Black life the next day after I learned that the police shot and killed two unarmed Black people in their vehicles.[2]

Police shot and killed LaTanya Haggerty, a 26 year-old graduate of Southern Illinois University and employee at Encyclopedia Britannica, Friday evening after one officer reportedly mistook her cell phone for a gun after a car chase. A few hours later, Chicago police officers shot and killed Robert Russ, a Northwestern University football player who, like me, was a senior nearing graduation. Police claimed that he struggled with them after he provoked a car chase. I was deeply disturbed by the news, but even more so by the lack of response from my Christian classmates. Unsurprisingly, as outsiders none of them knew anything about the shootings until I informed them. What did surprise me was their lack of interest. While these events awakened me to my vulnerability to police violence, my classmates seemed impervious to the most troubling aspects of these shootings. Months of protests followed the shootings, but I found that my white classmates were more likely to defend the police than to ask why Black people in Chicago, including me, were outraged.[3]

I left that summer with questions that have shaped my research into the history of American Christianity. How could my white Christian colleagues not be outraged by the violence of the police? What was it about my classmates, who often identified as "the Body of Christ," that allowed them to ignore their Black brother who informed them of the effect the incident had on his body without voicing any concern, except to defend the officers who were later fired?[4] Naively, I surmised that had police killed me—an honor roll, evangelical Christian college student, with no criminal record—my white classmates, and white America more broadly, would have reacted differently to the news. That response, I have come to understand, reflected a typical evangelical Christian belief that the politics of respectability would keep me safe. The politics of respectability suggest that, though I am Black, my evangelical Christian associations would have made my story more re-

2. Jennifer Vigil and James Janega, "2 Killed In Run-ins With City Police Victims' Families Demanding Answers," *Chicago Tribune*, June 6, 1999, http://articles.chicagotribune.com/1999-06-06/news/9906060235_1_chicago -police-latanya-haggerty-shooting.

3. Gary Marx and Terry Wilson, "3 Fired in Haggerty Case: Cops use of deadly force not warranted, board says," *Chicago Tribune*, March 18, 2000, http://articles.chicagotribune. com/2000-03-18/news/0003180082_1_police-board-latanya-haggerty-deadly-force.

4. The city of Chicago settled with Haggerty's family for 18 million dollars and settled with Russ's family for 9.6 million dollars.

spectable to white Americans than Haggerty's and Russ's and would have garnered outrage from white people who did not seem troubled by police violence against Black people.

In *Between the World and Me,* Ta-Nehisi Coates debunks the argument for the politics of respectability by presenting the story of his college friend as evidence. He reports that on September 1, 2000, a Prince George's County, MD, police officer shot and killed Prince Carmen Jones Jr., an unarmed Black, 25-year old Christian student at Howard University. While I experienced the murders of Haggerty and Russ vicariously, Coates was friends with Jones. After years of meditation, Coates reflected on the police murder to express concerns for his own son's safety:

> Prince Jones was the superlative of all my fears. And if he, good Christian, scion of a striving class, patron saint of the twice as good, could be forever bound, who then could not?[5]

Jones's murder was the antithesis of my belief in respectability politics. Jones's life epitomized respectability but that did not stop the officer from killing him. Nor did it inspire more than a few white evangelicals to question the systemic nature of police brutality against Black folk. Readers who were disappointed with the hopeless message in *Between the World and Me* seem to have missed that Coates's deep disappointment with America's hopeless legacy of destroying Black bodies was the occasion for writing the book in the first place.[6] An irony of the text's popularity and of the criticisms of its brief comments against hope is the failure of its readers to recognize what Coates articulates in the text: "A rage that burned in me then, animates me now, and will likely leave me on fire for the rest of my days" (83). Later he explains, "I didn't write the book thinking about [selling millions of copies]. My friend got killed, and I was deeply angry about that for a long time."[7]

Coates's heart-wrenching reflection on Jones's death reminded me of questions that arose for me in the summer of 1999. Why weren't more

5. Ta-Nehisi Coates, *Between the World and Me* (New York: Spiegel & Grau, 2015), 81.

6. Thabiti Anyabwile, "A Call for Hope in the Age of Mass Incarceration," *The Atlantic,* September 15, 2015, https://www.theatlantic.com/politics/archive/2015/09/why-there-needs-to-be-more-hope/404977/.

7. Ta-Nehisi Coates, "I'm a Big Believer in Chaos," Interview with Ezra Klein, *Vox,* December 19, 2016, http://www.vox.com/conversations/2016/12/19/13952578/ta-nehisi-coates-ezra-klein.

white Christians outraged by injustices against unarmed Black bodies? Why were so many white Christians quick to defend the officers in these situations? Coates's text was not written to address these questions, but his historical-ethical sensibilities offer helpful starting points for answering them. By building a historical-ethical lens centered on the Black body, Coates's text evoked the concept of racial Manicheanism—the process by which American Christians epidermalize light over darkness metaphors to justify white over Black racial hierarchies—which ideologically implicated the American Dream in killing Jones.[8] Coates implies that the Dream is more akin to a nightmare that is only made possible through the plunder of Black bodies. Coates uses the concept of "plunder" as shorthand for the stealing, trading, and enslaving of human bodies that built America. Apart from the oppressive imaginations of white Christians, this plunder would not have been possible. Their theology provided the moral justification for Americans to present the plunder of Black bodies as gospel, or good news.

Coates does not believe America is gospel. Instead, Coates writes of the nation as though it was a hypocritical religion full of contradictory beliefs. The historical record clearly shows that while the founding documents of the United States declare that all people were endowed by their Creator with equality and inalienable rights, the signatories meant something different by "all" when they exploited people of color's bodies to further the vision of white supremacy. Thus, Coates cannot believe in the American Dream, a dream predicated upon statecraft—"torture, theft, and enslavement"—because he values life in the body. "From an atheist perspective, life is precious—whenever someone dies, it's the end of their personal universe," Coates explains.[9] In this way, the Dream can never be anything more than a nightmare, because Dreamers tortured, stole, and enslaved Black bodies in their efforts to make it a reality.

> I have seen the dream all my life. It is perfect houses with nice lawns. It is Memorial Day cookouts, block associations, and driveways. The Dream is tree houses and Cub Scouts. The Dream smells like peppermint but tastes like strawberry shortcake. And for so long I have wanted to escape into the Dream, to fold my country over my head like a blanket. But this has never been an option because the Dream rests on our backs, the bedding made from our bodies. (11)

8. David Evans, "To Rid the Soul of One Dark Blot: Recognising Race in White Christian Religion," *Journal of Religious History* 39/3 (2015) 370–85.

9. Coates, "I'm a Big Believer in Chaos."

This is the key to understanding his interpretation of the American Dream, it has never been possible apart from the plunder of Black bodies.

Nor was the Dream possible apart from the moralizing authority that white Christian religion provided in justifying the plunder. Coates's use of religious language to describe American democracy, along with other passages, hints that white Protestantism is somehow implicated in plunder, but he does not provide much analysis of it. I am convinced that an analysis of the evangelistic efforts during colonial slavery demonstrates that the Christianization of theft, trade, and enslavement was an essential element of building the American Dream on the backs of Black people. The enduring nightmare of the American Dream is, at least in part, a result of the evangelical sanctification of the social inequities between Black enslaved people and white enslavers so that the latter could expand their ecclesial, political, and economic power. In what follows, I will discuss Coates's views on the national plunder that makes the myth of the American Dream possible. Then, I will narrate the theological innovations Christian missionaries used to endorse the plunder of Black bodies as gospel in the colonies. In so doing, I will show that evangelical Christians inherited a white Christianity that depends upon the exploitation of Black bodies and leaves its adherents impotent to challenge systemic racism.

DECONSTRUCTING THE DREAM

Like most Black Americans, Coates once loved the American Dream, but his love was short-lived.[10] Coates's reflection on the American Dream in his memoir, *The Beautiful Struggle,* symbolically foreshadows the elements that caused him to abandon the Dream in *Between the World and Me.* In the memoir, "The American Dream" is a large, charismatic, polka-dot-tight-wearing, blonde-haired, white professional wrestler named Dusty Rhodes who entered the ring to his theme song, "Common Man." Coates writes that while all of his young friends were fans of other wrestlers, for him "only the American Dream could endure."[11] But, Rhodes's common-man appeal and violent bravado could only endure Coates's immature adolescence.

10. According to the Aspen Institute, African Americans are the most likely demographic to believe the American Dream is more possible for them than for their parents; Aspen Institute, "The American Dream: Summary Report," 2015, https://www.slide-share.net/aspeninstitute/the-american-dream-summary-report

11. Ta-Nehisi Coates, *The Beautiful Struggle: A Memoir* (London: Verso, 2016), 5.

His father's life lessons on toil and struggle forced Coates to mature and confront the reality of the American Dream—that it, like professional wrestling, was a charade. Common people, like those from his neighborhood, did not often advance from rags to riches, no matter how hard they worked. Honorable people, like his father, lived most of their lives in obscurity. And no amount of respectable living could award Black people a Dream that was reserved for wealthy white people who were born into, or ascended to, the apex of Anglo-Saxon Protestantism. It troubled Coates that Dreamers did not recognize this reality; they believed instead "that their possession of the Dream is a natural result of grit, honor, and good works" (98).

Coates's father's Black-history lessons made it unlikely that his relationship with the American Dream could endure.[12] William Paul Coates was a curator at Howard University's Moorland-Spingarn Research Center and founder of Black Classic Press—a project to restore "out-of-print texts, obscure lectures, and self-published monographs" written by Black authors who recorded Black history at a time when academia hardly recognized Black America had a history to record. The Press embodied the belief system he hoped to instill in Black families across the United States, that the intelligence and gifts of the African Diaspora could overcome white America's oppressive power. The Press influenced everyone in the Coates family. Ta-Nehisi Coates recalls seeing the dire statistics on Black men often quoted and recited in newspapers his father left around the house "1 in 21 killed by 1 in 21, more of us in jail than in college."[13] His father, influenced by Jawanza Kunjufu, provided informal education to counter the conspiracy to destroy his Black children.[14] He introduced him to the works of J. C. Degraft Johnson, Marcus Garvey, Malcolm X, and others from the Black nationalist tradition. This stream of Black nationalism ran counter to the American Christian nationalism of figures like Martin Luther King Jr. and Shirley Chisolm, who engaged national politics in hopes that every Black American could achieve the Dream.

Coates eventually decided that he needed to replace the American Dream with his own dreams because the American Dream was inimical to the work of his life. He discovered, however, that even his dreams were problematic:

12. Coates, *Beautiful Struggle*, 14.
13. Coates, *Beautiful Struggle*, 7.
14. Coates, *Beautiful Struggle*, 8.

> The Dream thrives on generalization, on limiting the number of possible questions, on privileging immediate answers. The Dream is the enemy of all art, courageous thinking, and honest writing. And it became clear that this was not just for the dreams concocted by Americans to justify themselves but also for the dreams that I had concocted to replace them. (50)

Whether Black or white, religious or secular, Americans of every stripe were susceptible to the abstract allure of the "rags to riches" myth and other immaterial hopes. The demonstrative presentation and pervasiveness of the Dream provided no space for other dreams and by definition devalued Black and brown dreams. Moreover, Coates found that all abstractions, dreams disconnected from historical realities, were limiting and lacked courage. In Coates's view, even Black and brown dreams stifled courageous thought and honest writing.

Many Black southerners who sought the American Dream migrated to northern cities like St. Louis, Chicago, Detroit, New York, and Baltimore, and were influenced by cultural traditions that annexed Black politics to the Christian sacred cosmos. William Paul Coates, however, was not raised on the tradition of the Black Church struggle for freedom and justice. Thus, he raised his son on a Black nationalist tradition that taught him to be skeptical of faith in a divine destiny for American statecraft. Ta-Nehisi Coates returned to that lesson later in life, but this time with a critique that included "racecraft." It was a critique that espoused faith in the destiny of the Black race, but it too was metaphysical. "My great error was not that I had accepted someone else's dream but that I had accepted the fact of dreams, the need for escape," he wrote (56). And it was this recognition that made him doubt the efficacy of his and all dreams, "Perhaps I too had the capacity for plunder" (60).

While Coates's faith in the Dream was short lived, the legacy of the Dream has a long history. According to Jim Cullen, author of *The American Dream: History of an Idea that Shaped a Nation*, the phrase "American Dream" first gained prominence after 1931 when James Truslow Adams argued, in *The Epic of America*, "that the American dream of a better richer and happier life for all our citizens of every rank. . . is the greatest contribution we have made to the thought and welfare of the world. That dream or hope has been present from the start."[15] Cullen suggests that the

---

15. James Truslow Adams, *The Epic of America* (New Brunswick, NJ: Transaction, 2012), xx.

idea rests on a premise that colonial settlers, founders of the republic, and nineteenth-century immigrants shared: that America is a land of divine providence, expansionist destiny, and economic opportunity. Hope in the Dream provided those who could legally claim United States citizenship with the national and spiritual fortitude to persist in the American state-making project, despite the cost of human lives their vision required.

Like Charles Tilly who argued that state-making "qualifies as our largest example of organized crime," Coates calls into question the American Dream on account of its inherent toleration of the criminal acts required to make America a reality. According to Tilly, coercive exploitation is central to the practice of creating nation-states: "Banditry, piracy, gangland rivalry, policing, and war making all belong on the same continuum."[16] Coates's insight that the plunder of Black bodies was crucial to the creation of America undoubtedly belongs on that spectrum.

A new generation of Dreamers has either not considered the thesis of plunder or has rejected it. They seem to agree, instead, with the views of America's first Black president, Barack Obama, particularly when he beseeched all Americans "to realize that your dreams do not have to come at the expense of my dreams; that investing in the health, welfare, and education of Black and brown and white children will ultimately help all of America prosper."[17] Coates has frequently found Obama's lack of systemic analysis problematic.[18] That is because the president's description of the Dream is out of step with millions of Americans whose racial caste locks them out of economically stable neighborhoods, marks them as future inmates rather than brilliant minds, and traps them in cycles of debt. Believers in the Dream, like Obama, apparently do not recognize that too often suburban dreams of safety have come at the expense of targeting Black men, who are three times more likely to be recipients of police force than their white counter parts.[19] The idea that the American Dream is equally

16. Charles Tilly, "War Making and State Making as Organized Crime," in *Bringing the State Back In*, ed. Peter B. Evans et al. (Cambridge: Cambridge University Press, 1985), 171–73.

17. Barack Obama, "Sen. Barack Obama Addresses Race at the Constitution Center in Philadelphia," *Washington Post*, March 18, 2008, http://www.washingtonpost.com/wp-dyn/content/article/2008/03/18/AR2008031801081.html?sid=ST2008031801183.

18. Coates, "My President was Black," *The Atlantic*, January/February 2017, https://www.theatlantic.com/magazine/archive/2017/01/my-president-was-black/508793/.

19. Timothy Williams, "Study Supports Suspicion That Police Are More Likely to Use Force on Blacks," *New York Times*, July 7, 2016, http://www.nytimes.com/2016/07/08/us/study-supports-suspicion-that-police-use-of-force-is-more-likely-for-Blacks.html.

available to all ignores the over 70-billion-dollar prison-industrial complex that grows at the expense of equitable education for Black and brown students.[20] Moreover, the growing net-worth disparity between white and Black families challenges the notion that white Americans can realize the Dream without exploiting Black and brown bodies.[21] The historical record demonstrates that whatever people believe the American Dream to be, the quest for it has always come at the expense of Black and brown people.

Coates does not include Black Americans in the population of Dreamers. Interestingly, the demographic most likely to believe in the promise of the American Dream according to a 2012 survey are Black Americans. As of 2015, 55 percent of Black folk, a higher percentage than hispanic (52 percent) or white Americans (35 percent), believe it is easier for them to achieve the American Dream than their parents.[22] Coates is one of 45 percent of Black Americans who does not fit that category. Since 1963, when Martin Luther King Jr. preached, "I have a dream deeply rooted in the American Dream," many Black Christians dreamed that they too could cash in on America's promise of "unalienable rights" of "life, liberty, and the pursuit of happiness" for all. Despite the many ways that America defaulted on its "promissory note," King implored his beloved community, "to refuse to believe that the bank of justice is bankrupt."[23]

While many may have heeded King's request, the relationship between Black America and the American Dream vacillates between longing and condemnation. Langston Hughes poem "Let America be America Again" is indicative of this ambivalent relationship. The mid-twentieth century poem is a plea from the voice of one who desires the dream but accuses America of never having lived up to it:

20. Tracie R. Porter, "The School-to-Prison Pipeline: The Business Side of Incarcerating, Not Educating, Students in Public Schools," *Arkansas Law Review* 68:1 (2015), http://media.law.uark.edu/arklawreview/2015/05/15/the-school-to-prison-pipeline-the-business-side-of-incarcerating-not-educating-students-in-public-schools/.

21. Joshua Holland, "The Average Black Family Would Need 228 Years to Build the Wealth of a White Family Today," *The Nation*, August 8, 2016, https://www.thenation.com/article/the-average-Black-family-would-need-228-years-to-build-the-wealth-of-a-white-family-today/.

22. Tammy Luhby, "Why Blacks Believe in the American Dream More than Whites," CNN Money, November 25, 2015, http://money.cnn.com/2015/11/24/news/economy/race-american-dream/index.html?iid=EL.

23. King, "I Have a Dream," March on Washington, August 28, 1963, https://www.archives.gov/files/press/exhibits/dream-speech.pdf.

Let it be the dream it used to be.
Let it be the pioneer on the plain
Seeking a home where he himself is free.
(America never was America to me.)[24]

James Presley has suggested that for Hughes the American Dream was "the raison d'etre of this nation."[25] Hughes concludes the poem with a hopeful investment in the Dream, "America will be!" It is a hope shared by many Black Americans.

Despite the Dream's devastating effects on Black folk from the Early Republic to the Age of Obama, many Black Christians who migrated from the Jim Crow south adopted its vision of embourgeoisement and the traditional values of middle-class Protestantism that came with it.[26] By adopting these values, they believed that their hard work and full participation in Protestant Christianity would earn them the Dream. But the suffering of Black bodies sharply contradicted the products the Dream promised. By placing Black bodies in the center of his interpretation of American history, Coates offers his readers an alternative to an unexamined allegiance to the Dream that was created for white America and baptized in white Protestant Christianity.

Ralph Ellison who, like Coates, was a Black atheist and fierce critic of the American Dream bemoaned that for Black Americans the "dream contained a strong dose of such stuff as nightmares are made of."[27] Ellison explained, "By excluding our largest minority from the democratic process the United States has weakened all national symbols and rendered sweeping public rituals which would dramatize the American dream impossible."[28] Ellison's nineteenth-century critique is a reminder that Coates's body ethic is part of a long tradition. Black social critics have consistently challenged the nobility of the American Dream on account of this ethic. Malcolm X, who often exhorted his audiences to love their flesh, rebuked the entire notion of a dream, "We don't see any American dream. We've experienced

24. Langston Hughes, "Let America Be America," In *The Collected Poems of Langston Hughes,* ed. Arnold Rampersad, et al. (New York: Vintage, 1995), 189–90.

25. James Presley, "The American Dream of Langston Hughes," *Southwest Review* 48, no. 4 (Autumn 1963): 380–86.

26. Albert J. Raboteau, *African-American Religion* (New York: Oxford University Press, 1999), 69.

27. Ellison, *Shadow,* 304.

28. Ellison, *Shadow,* 36.

only the American nightmare."[29] James Baldwin also protested that "the American dream has become something much more closely resembling a nightmare."[30] King, too, only a few years after preaching "I have a dream," feared it had "turned into a nightmare."[31] More recently, Jesse Jackson added a similar fear that "Dr. King's Dream is in danger of becoming a modern American nightmare."[32] From Coates's historical perspective, the Dream was always a nightmare for Black people and nothing good came from its creation.

THE GOOD NEWS OF AMERICAN PLUNDER

The reality that Black bodies labored for a vision that has not benefitted them or their progeny makes any ambivalence that Black Americans have about the Dream understandable. White Protestant Christians generally do not share this ambivalence. That is due, in no small part, to white Protestant Christianity's complicity in Christianizing the institution of slavery. When white Protestant evangelists encountered white enslavers reluctant to Christianize enslaved people in the eighteenth century, they developed theological tools that Christianized the oppression of Black bodies. By theologically bifurcating body from soul, they produced ecclesial practices that endorsed enslaving Black people. Though they were confronted with contradictions inherent to the slave system when they preached about religious liberty, economic and hierarchical interests inspired them to justify enslaving Black and brown bodies to secure the prosperity of wealthy white people. This justification was especially necessary for white Christians who allowed Black people to become members of their church body while defending their state-given right to buy and sell Black human bodies as property so they could pursue the Dream.

White colonial American Christians who advocated for liberty had to contend with the reality that their Dream of freedom and economic

---

29. Malcolm X, "The Bullet or the Ballot," Cleveland, Ohio, April, 3, 1964. In *Speeches That Reshaped the World*, ed. Alan J Whiticker (Sydney: New Holland, 2009), 267–71.

30. James Baldwin, *The Fire Next Time* (New York: Vintage Books, 1993), 87.

31. The Daily Nightly, "King in 1967: My dream has 'turned into a nightmare,'" August 27, 2013, http://www.nbcnews.com/news/other/king-1967-my-dream-has-turned-nightmare-f8C11013179.

32 Jesse Jackson, "Affirmative Action is a Majority Issue that Benefits Everybody," October 27, 1997, Sacramento, CA, http://www.inmotionmagazine.com/jjsave.html.

prosperity depended on enslaving other human beings, an action that often contradicted their understanding of good Christian behavior. Undeterred by the contradictions, Christian evangelists toiled to make enslavement morally consistent with the Dream. In his text, *American Slavery, American Freedom*, the historian Edmund Morgan argues that by juxtaposing freedom with slavery, the two ideas grew together "the one supporting the other."[33] Morgan did not demonstrate, however, how essential Evangelical religion was to sanctifying this union. Evangelists endorsed the subjugation, oppression, pillaging, and enslavement of American Africans and American Indians. Evangelical complicity in and endorsement of such practices made Christianity essential to the ongoing legacy of the Dream, because without Christianity's complicity and endorsement the plunder of these bodies would not have been morally justifiable.

Evangelists reconciled the conflict between slavery and freedom by creating liturgical practices and theological arguments that reduced the religious value of enslaved bodies, all the while building the economy with their labor. To do this, white evangelists used the concept of spiritual liberty to keep the physical value of the enslaved to the enslaver intact. Coates claims that such actions are heretical to American Democracy. The eighteenth-century journals and letters of evangelists Francis Le Jau and George Whitefield, however, suggest that at these early stages of American colonization Christian missionaries concocted a public Christian orthodoxy that turned theft, torture, and enslavement into gospel for white enslavers. Missionaries of this new orthodoxy had the ecclesial and social power to persuade enslavers, who were reluctant to Christianize enslaved people, that Christianizing enslaved populations would make enslavers wealthier. Evangelists, like Whitefield, even persuaded colonies that previously prohibited slavery to change their laws so that the Dream could become a possibility for white Americans at the expense of Black people and their descendants.

Sociologists Michael Emerson and Christian Smith argue that eighteenth-century evangelical views on slavery were complicated, because while white Christians argued both against and for enslaving Africans they "believed that the mission of the church, seen as evangelizing and discipling, must come first." This evangelism-first ethic did not, however, supersede the material privileges and social power white evangelicals gained

33. Edmund Morgan, *American Slavery, American Freedom* (New York: Norton, 2003), 6.

from the system. According to Emerson and Smith, "[evangelicals] usually fail to challenge the system not just out of concern for evangelism, but also because they support the American system and enjoy its fruits."[34] There is much to affirm in this interpretation, but it implies that evangelicals merely enjoy whatever spoils they may gain from the system when more accurately their theology requires the system to provide them with power and privileges. The narratives of Francis LeJau in the Carolinas and George Whitefield in Georgia demonstrate that evangelicals not only supported the system because evangelicals "enjoy its fruits," they also created a theology to justify it which allowed them to claim the American Dream as their own.

Le Jau and Whitefield represent the evolution of an evangelical orthodoxy that justified the plunder of Black bodies in Colonial America. Le Jau represents the development of an explicit theological justification for enslaving Black people, while Whitefield represents the application of this theology towards the expansion of exploiting Black bodies for white people's gain. This orthodoxy was pervasive in colonial American evangelical Christian life, so much so that divergent Black and white forms of Christianity emerged from the crucible of the slave system: Black churches as therapeutic temples and activist organizations against the trauma of enslavement, and white churches as sanctuaries for enslavers and other white beneficiaries of slavery to praise the source from whom they gained their gift of plunder.

Francis Le Jau was a missionary of the Society of the Propagation of the Gospel in Goose Creek, South Carolina, from 1706 to 1717 who pioneered a theological intervention that would undergird future Christian defenses for slavery. The Anglican Church tasked him with converting as many in the settlement as possible, including enslaved Africans and Indigenous people. After he noted the objections enslavers voiced against converting Africans, he made reconciling the system of slavery to evangelism and discipleship his primary theological task. White enslavers were not keen on allowing Africans to attend religious instruction, because enslavers believed that baptism might manumit slaves or at least make them less productive.

The idea that baptism freed enslaved people was widespread in the colonies. This was due in part to questions colonists had concerning whether English law permitted Christians to be enslaved.[35] "So persistent

---

34. Michael O. Emerson and Christian Smith, *Divided by Faith: Evangelical Religion and the Problem of Race in America* (New York: Oxford University Press, 2001), 29.

35. Jessica M. Parr., *Inventing George Whitefield: Race, Revivalism, and the Making of a Religious Icon* (Jackson: University of Mississippi, 2015), 3.

was this idea," according to historian Edgar Pennington, "that letters were dispatched from London on the subject, and special laws were passed in certain colonies, in order to assure the slaveowner that there was no ground for apprehension."[36] Colonists may also have perceived what Albert Raboteau calls "the egalitarianism implicit in Christianity," that conversion transformed even people of no relation into Christian kinfolk.[37] How could one enslave a brother or sister? For colonial enslavers who taught that Africans and Indians were "beasts, and use them like such," Le Jau had to convince them that Africans could be both humans with souls and enslaved as Christians.[38] This was an enormous task because any action that threatened to make enslaved and enslaver equal destabilized the moral grounds upon which the slave system stood.

White enslavers were also reticent to Christianize enslaved Africans because they believed that they would not be productive. Le Jau could not find reasons for another issue he called "new opposition" to his catechetical instruction; he surmised that it was due to "the old pretext that baptism makes the slaves proud and undutiful." Le Jau also reinforced the accusation that enslaved Christians would be undutiful when he began keeping them after the Sunday service for catechism, resulting in less available labor for the enslavers.[39]

Le Jau addressed the enslaver's first concern by adding a liturgical agreement to the baptism of enslaved Africans:

> You declare in the Presence of God and before this Congregation that you do not ask for the holy baptism out of any design to ffree [sic] yourself from the Duty and Obedience you owe to your Master while you live, but meerly [sic] for the good of Your soul and to partake of the Graces and Blessings promised to the Members of the Church of Jesus Christ.[40]

---

36. Edgar Legare Pennington, "The Reverend Francis Le Jau's Work Among Indians and Negro Slaves," *The Journal of Southern History*, Vol. 1, No. 4 (November 1935): 455.

37. Albert J.Raboteau, *Slave Religion: The Invisible Institution in the Antebellum South* (Oxford: Oxford University Press, 2004), 102.

38. Francis Le Jau, "Slave Conversion on the Carolina Frontier: June 13, 1710," in *African American Religious History: A Documentary Witness* ed. Milton C. Sernett (Duke University Press, Durham 1999), 29.

39. Le Jau, "Slave Conversion on the Carolina Frontier," 30.

40. Le Jau, "Slave Conversion on the Carolina Frontier," 26.

Le Jau's instruction concerning enslavement was unusual in that it directly addressed the enslaved population. The Anglican church usually attempted to alleviate the concerns of enslavers by sending letters that instructed enslavers to Christianize enslaved people without fear that those actions would result in their manumission. In a letter "to the masters and mistresses of families in the English plantations abroad," the Bishop of London exhorted enslavers "to consider [slaves], not merely as slaves upon the same level with labouring beasts, but as men-slaves and women-slaves, who have the same frame and faculties with yourselves, and have souls capable of being made eternally happy and reason and understanding to receive instruction in order to it."[41] Alternatively, Le Jau's liturgical proclamation simultaneously addressed both the enslaved and enslaver under the authority of the Anglican church, thereby subjugating the enslaved, assuring the enslaver of that subjugation, and claiming the authority of the Anglican church through the sacrament. The baptismal liturgy theologically bifurcated the Black body from the soul; it declared that what baptism set free in the soul was not true for the body. Moreover, because the liturgical statement was applied only to Black people, it sanctified the social inequities between the Black and white population.

Le Jau also sanctified enslavers' concerns about the work ethic of enslaved Africans. He reported that they "idly and criminally" spent time when they worked outside the watchful eye of white enslavers. He found no merit, however, to the idea that Christianity would make them idler and "endeavored to convince them of the contrary." To this end, he made his enslaved catechumens promise that they would "spend no more than the Lord's day in idleness." As would become routine for Christian evangelists in the eighteenth and nineteenth centuries, he argued that Christian teaching aided in the enslavement process. Le Jau implored his parish to have faith that those he baptized would "behave themselves very well," even to the point that they would alert Le Jau to any plot of enslaved people to free themselves. Moreover, he endeared his evangelistic efforts to enslavers' economic interests by claiming that enslaved Christians "do better for their masters profit than formerly, for they are taught to serve out of Christian love and duty."[42]

Like Le Jau, other evangelists were sympathetic to white enslavers' concerns for profits. Only a few decades later, "the Great Awakening"

41. Raboteau, *Slave Religion*, 101.
42. Le Jau, "Slave Conversion on the Carolina Frontier," 26, 29.

British evangelist, George Whitefield, confronted enslavers with his desire to preach the gospel to enslaved Africans in America. Whitefield had led the Methodist revivals in England that were activated by the scandal of open-air preaching to crowds upwards of tens of thousands. As a first generation Methodist whose Christian faith criticized the dead orthodoxy of the Anglican Church, his brand of preaching was new to the colonies and contributed to making him the most popular evangelist of his generation.

When he traveled to the American colonies, he continued to preach to masses, but he insisted that he would only continue to do so if he was also allowed to preach to enslaved Africans. Historian Jessica Parr writes, "Whitefield was well known for his caustic 1740 rebuke of southern (mostly Anglican) planters for their poor treatment of their slaves, and more particularly for their failure to ensure their religious instruction."[43] Similarly to Le Jau, this early evangelical pop-star's views on enslaved Africans challenged notions that Christianity was incompatible with enslavers' economic interests. Whitefield advanced the theological idea that freedom for enslaved people's souls in the after-life would make their bodies profitable for enslavers in the here-and-now. By converting enslaved people to Christianity, enslavers would be able to use ecclesial authority, bible verses, and the implicit sense that the social order was divinely ordained to better control them.

By the time Whitefield reached the colonies, the debate over Christianizing enslaved Africans was well under way; he supported Christianizing them. Not all colonies shared in the debate over Christianizing enslaved Africans, because not all colonies legalized slavery at the same time.[44] This became an issue for Whitefield when he dreamed of working with white orphans in the colony of Georgia, because it prohibited slavery until 1751. Like other evangelical preachers, Whitefield had no problem arguing for the economic profitability of slaveholding. In 1741, only a year after he rebuked numerous southern states for their poor treatment of enslaved people, he argued that Georgia needed to change its laws to accommodate his desire to build an orphanage in the colony:

> As for manuring more land than the hired servants and great boys can manage, it is impracticable without a few negroes.[45]

43. Parr, *Inventing George Whitefield*, 5.

44. Massachusetts was the first colony to legalize slavery in 1641.

45. George Whitefield, "Bethesda, December 23, 1741," in *A Select Collection of Letters of the Late Reverend George Whitefield, M.A. of Pembroke-College, Oxford, and Chaplain to the Rt. Hon. the Countess of Huntingdon ; Written to His Most Intimate Friends, and*

Whitefield's desire to enslave Africans to build a house for white orphans once again brings into question the contention that white dreams did not need to come at the expense of Black dreams.

In a 1741 letter he wrote concerning the orphanage he named Bethesda, Whitefield explained that God had inspired his vision. "I think, with a full assurance of faith that the Lord put it into my heart to build that house," he wrote. He envisioned that Bethesda would be "a house of mercy to the souls and bodies of many people, both old and young."[46] As he made plans for the orphanage, his heart for charity grew to include people of all ages. However, his vision for old and young bodies and souls did not extend to the bodies of Black people. Legalizing slavery in Georgia meant that Black bodies would live their lives in forced servitude, as would their progeny. Building Whitefield's dream of prosperity for white girls, boys, women, and men came at the expense of Black girls, boys, women, and men.

Scholars have too often emphasized Whitefield's eagerness to share his evangelical message of sin and salvation for all and minimized their critique of his fervor for enslaving Black bodies. Christian historian Thomas Kidd, for example, minimizes Whitefield's views on slavery by arguing that he reflected the views of most of his evangelical contemporaries. The problem with this explanation is that Kidd does not consider the objections to slavery of the Black converts themselves. That only a few white Christians were on record voicing their objections to slavery demonstrates a failure to seriously consider Black Christian objections to enslavement when there can be little doubt that the laws created to keep people enslaved implied that by and large Blacks did not approve of the chains that bound them to labor for white society.[47] As we have seen, Whitefield had no problem challenging prevailing notions that contradicted his Christian ideals. Still, he never advocated for the manumission of slaves or the abolition of the institution of slavery; instead, he called for enslavers to treat enslaved Africans less harshly. Such an exhortation suggests that he concerned his theology primarily with protecting the economic interests of enslavers and white people in general—a concern that he surmised could only be secured by exploiting Black bodies even when it was prohibited.

Persons of Distinction, in England, Scotland, Ireland, and America, from the Year 1734, to 1770. Including the Whole Period of His Ministry. With an Account of the Orphan-House in Georgia, to the Time of His Death (London: Edward and Charles Dilly, 1772), 435.

46. Whitefield, "Bethesda," 431.

47. Thomas Kidd, *George Whitefield* (New Haven: Yale University Press, 2014), 189.

CONCLUSION

White Christian sanctification of plunder made the American Dream a nightmare for Black and brown people. Though initially, plunder, in the form of enslavement, posed contradictions to white enslavers' sense of morality, white missionaries alleviated that tension by creating new liturgies, by interpreting biblical passages, and by constructing theological arguments that justified exploiting Black bodies. In this way, Christianity was complicit in creating a dream for white people that could only be realized at the expense of the dreams of Black and brown people.

As a Black atheist, Coates could not put any faith in the American Dream, and his text, *Between the World and Me,* condemns it as the idea that took the life of his friend Prince Jones. Certainly, white readers could sympathize with his grief, but many could not understand his rage against the Dream because their white identity rested in its rewards, rewards their ancestors intended solely for them. As a young college student at a predominately white institution, I failed to realize how dependent my white Christian college classmates were on the Dream. As such, they were ill-equipped, historically or spiritually, to embrace my rage at a system constructed to secure their dreams and justify the murders of Haggerty and Russ. My reaction threatened their belief in the American Dream upon which their white Christian identity relied. Their inability to identify with my outrage awakened me to the truth of the American Dream: for people of color, the Dream is a nightmare from which neither respectability politics nor evangelical faith can save.

6

WHAT DOES HE MEAN BY, "THEY BELIEVE THEY ARE WHITE"?

— REGGIE WILLIAMS —

Ta-Nehisi Coates's very popular book is a lengthy, three-part letter to his son, which could make it a difficult target for theological analysis of this sort. Yet, this is no ordinary father/son conversation. This heart-to-heart is written in light of the bloodshed that makes necessary "the talk" that black parents must have with our children in a nation where black people have historically been robbed by state representatives of the right to exclusive possession of our own bodies. Arguments that invoke black-on-black violence as a rebuttal to protests about police brutality overlook the fact that we should have the right to expect the state to value our lives as it does the lives of everyone else. Yet, black people, Coates argues, face the constant threat of having our bodies "plundered," as "any claim to ourselves, to the hands that secured us, the spine that braced us, and the head that directed us, [is] contestable."[1] As a result of this grim reality for black people in the U.S., Coates's conversation with his son is not merely private and personal; it is an important part of black communal life.

---

1. Ta-Nehisi Coates, *Between the World and Me* (New York: Spiegel and Grau, 2015), 37.

The title of the book is taken from Richard Wright's gripping poem of the same name. Wright's poem "Between the World and Me" (1935) narrates the shock of a person who stumbles upon the still-smoldering aftermath of a lynching while taking a morning stroll in the woods. The imagery is intense; a simple morning walk illuminated by sunlight through tree branches is violently arrested by the discovery of human bones lying on top of a heap of hot ashes; the lynchers' cigars, cigarettes, and lipstick mingled together with the blood-soaked clothing of their victim, lying nearby. The ghastly discovery is indicative of life for black people in the brutally racist United States where the specter of lynching lingers, and day-to-day life is haunted by apprehensions about when, where, and who will be next. An untold number of black bodies continues to be added to the cloud of witnesses whose plight is testimony to the inhumanity of racism, as murdered black people proliferate in what appears to be an enduring orgy of white lust for black blood. The shock of the chilling encounter in the woods provokes the poem's un-named narrator to re-live the horrific event with the murdered victim, which in turn places the reader inside of the terror from the victim's perspective, through the narrator's imagination and the poem's visceral imagery:

And while I stood my mind was frozen within cold pity
   for the life that was gone.
The ground gripped my feet and my heart was circled by
   icy walls of fear—
The sun died in the sky; a night wind muttered in the
   grass and fumbled the leaves in the trees; the woods
   poured forth the hungry yelping of hounds; the
   darkness screamed with thirsty voices; and the witnesses rose and lived:
The dry bones stirred, rattled, lifted, melting themselves
   into my bones.
The grey ashes formed flesh firm and black, entering into
   my flesh.
The gin-flask passed from mouth to mouth, cigars and
   cigarettes glowed, the whore smeared lipstick red
   upon her lips,
And a thousand faces swirled around me, clamoring that
   my life be burned . . .

Coates invokes the poem's dissonance between sensible day-to-day existence and fears of unfettered white violence that have been all too familiar for black life in the United States. Fears, Coates explains, that result from the war waged between white yearning for an imaginary ideal place and actual life with people in the real world. In a poignant segment early in the letter Coates re-narrates a dialogue with his son after it was announced that the killers of Michael Brown would not be indicted. The killers left eighteen-year-old Michael's dead body in a Ferguson, Missouri, street for hours, "like some awesome declaration of their inviolable power,"[2] and they would not be held accountable for treating him and his community in that way. Coates reminds his son that he waited up until 11:00 p.m. for an announcement that was not what he'd hoped for, and it sent him to his room in tears. Rather than hug his crying son, Coates coached him with the talk, "this is your country . . . this is your world, . . . this is your body, and you must find some way to live within the all of it."[3] Later in the book, he indicates why he would not hug his son, "The struggle is really all I have for you because it is the only portion of this world under your control. I am sorry that I cannot make it okay. I am sorry that I cannot save you—but not that sorry."[4] When the justice system refused to indict Michael Brown's killers, Coates's son made contact with what Coates describes as the fears that are familiar staples of black life in the U.S. They are fears that color all areas of black life, from parenting norms to dating regulations, clothing styles, style of music, all of these elements within the black community of Coates's formation included a catalogue of responses to a life infused with fears of state-sanctioned racist violence against black people in the United States. The long shadow of racism lingers over the nation and is cause for the persistent yearning of white supremacy that Coates identifies as "the Dream."

Coates's rendition of "Between the World and Me" is written in the style of the opening essay in James Baldwin's *The Fire Next Time*. Baldwin's essay is a letter to his nephew titled "My Dungeon Shook: Letter to my Nephew on the 100th Anniversary of the Emancipation." Coates's analysis moves around two poles: the dangerous white "dream" at the core of an American fantasy and the memory of his time at his alma mater, Howard University, as what he calls "the Mecca." The point of this talk with his son is not to ground his understanding of himself in a more accurate representation, not to know "who you really are," to quote Countee Cullen's "Hey Black Child," but simply to affirm his son's struggle against the Dream. Yet, I find Coates's words to his son about the struggle, as "all I have for you," to

2. Coates, *Between the World and Me*, 11.

3. Coates, *Between the World and Me*, 12.

4. Coates, *Between the World and Me*, 107.

be problematic and worthy of a prolonged engagement. In this brief essay I will offer a few interactive thoughts.

PROBLEMATIZING THE STRUGGLE

This white "dream" that Coates refers to is a familiar longing that informs how we know one another in the Western world, but it is not about a lust for black blood. Indeed, it has very little to do with black people. As Coates describes it, the Dream for white people is "gorgeous." "It is perfect houses and nice lawns. It is Memorial Day cookouts, block associations, and driveways. The Dream is tree houses and the Cub Scouts. The Dream smells like peppermint but tastes like strawberry shortcake."[5] The Dream is, in fact, about white space, and white community; a psychic escape into longing for a place like the fictional village in the television show "Little House on the Prairie," or The Andy Griffith Show's "Mayberry." These fictional white spaces—artistically rendered in media, arts, and academia—illustrate the persistent longing that sets the imagination of a white watching world towards an idealized community populated with idealized humanity that is calibrated by the template of idealized white, often wealthy, masculinity. The effect of calibrating humanity according to an idealized template is to render "human being" as a hegemonic term, for whites only. The idealized inhabitants of Mayberry, for example, suggest a community that is a peaceful, moral world, where the police have little if any work to do, crime and poverty are unheard of, and white men are in charge. People are reasonable in this idyllic space, and they care for one another on a first-name basis. What happens to black people as a result of the white longing for Mayberry is a secondary effect of "the Dream."

The physical absence of such a place is registered by whiteness as a crisis and nostalgia for an imaginary bygone era. James Baldwin makes reference to the Dream while writing about a white friendship, "I am afraid that most of the white people I have ever known impressed me as being in the grip of a weird nostalgia, dreaming of a vanished state of security and order . . . the troubles of white people failed to impress me as being real trouble."[6] The fictionalized bygone idyllic is not real trouble because it is grounded in the conceptual, on an ideal. It is ideology, not reality, that motivates white

5. Coates, *Between the World and Me*, 10.

6. James Baldwin, *Nobody Knows My Name: More Notes of a Native Son* (New York: Dial, 1961), 217–18.

grasping to recover and stabilize themselves in their imagination of white space. It is symptomatic of the problem that Baldwin identifies with protest novels: "[T]hey are a mirror of our confusion, dishonesty, panic, trapped and immobilized in the sunlit prison of an American dream. They are fantasies, connecting nowhere with reality, sentimental . . . ."[7]

The Dream is also animated by theology that shapes the collective interpretation of human being according to the ideological longing for white space. It is religious-inflected, ideological incentive for violence against minoritized humanity, who are aesthetically different than the idealized type, and whose presence represents a threat to the ideal. The distress over its imagined passing is theoretical justification for the trouble heaped upon the bodies of people of color. In the Dream, the ground appears to be shifting under the feet of the white dreamer, and efforts to stabilize the Dream are drastic, they are violent, and they are levied with righteous indignation. In effect, dark bodies are sacrificed to appease white adoration of the Dream. Longing for Mayberry becomes incentive for cruelty, which betrays the Dream as little more than ideological justification for murder. Hence, it matters to examine the notion of "the struggle" in greater detail to properly diagnose what we must address, and how to best help awaken white folks from their dreams.

WHAT DOES IT MEAN TO BELIEVE IN THE DREAM?

Coates describes this dream by making use of the terms "belief," and "believers," and he speaks of a deified Democracy, and of "Mecca,"[8] all the while intentionally omitting engagement with the significance of these religious terms within his argument. His reference to God invokes his emphasis on fear, ". . . I am afraid. And I have no God to hold me up. And I believe that when they shatter the body they shatter everything, and I knew that all of us—Christians, Muslims, atheists—lived in this fear of this truth."[9] Although this apparent reference to God is a description of the absence of confessional convictions for himself and his family, the language of belief looms large and un-interrogated inside of his analysis of the Dream and its impact on society. His description of black life in the United States ignores an inevitable engagement with the religious that informs social life for both

7. Baldwin, *Nobody Knows My Name*, 16.

8. Coates, *Between the World and Me*, 6–7.

9. Coates, *Between the World and Me*, 113.

black and white people. It is an engagement that he could not avoid, even while addressing his son as he sat crying in emotional distress on his bed. Coates made a decision about which hope he would offer his crying son, upon the realization that the justice system chose to value Michael Brown's killers and not Michael Brown's humanity, or the humanity of his black Missouri community. As a personal admonition to his son, his response to that moment of grief is gripping, while he narrates his decision about how he will engage the traditions available to him within the struggle.

This prolonged narrative is critical analysis of a people who believe they are white, understood as ideal, whose dream of a white world produces ideological validation to devalue some human lives in adulation of ideal human life. Black people in the United States have a history of struggle against white people's dreams, as Coates identifies. But the struggle for black people in the U.S. also includes aspirations for freedom and co-humanity articulated by other dreamers, like Harriet Tubman, Sojourner Truth, Ida B. Wells-Barnett, Joanne Robinson, Claudette Colvin, and the Rev. Dr. Martin Luther King Jr. Those dreams, the white one and black ones, are significantly different, yet they are tethered to hope inspired by religious confessions. How is the language of belief at work within these religion-inspired dreams? Because the notion of a dream that informs our daily life in society for both black and white people is buttressed by basic convictions of what it means to be human, and the nature of Christian discipleship, it is clear that one cannot interact in any substantial way with problems of identity like race, as articulated in *Between the World and Me*, without interaction with the religious beliefs inside of the Dream that inspires white supremacy and with the religious worldview that informs black resistance.

THE CONNECTION BETWEEN WHITE AND DIVINE

W. E. B. Du Bois understood this point over a century ago. He argued that a fundamental antagonism to black life in the United States is the way that race has profoundly shaped our understanding of the divine and of who counts as fully human. In his groundbreaking book *The Souls of Black Folk* published in 1903, Du Bois conveys to his readers that there is a fundamental difference between the way white people view black people and the way that black people view ourselves. The crux of this difference is illustrated by two connected metaphors that Du Bois describes as the veil and double consciousness. The veil is an opaque feature of the white racial imagination that covers black people, only allowing whites to see what they imagine black people to be—the Negro as epitomized by the imagination of a self-defined, watching, white world. The resulting experience for black people behind the veil is double consciousness understood as two un-reconciled identities, American and Negro. They represent the impulse to be acknowledged as a fellow citizen and contributing member of mainstream society, and the impulse to reject white racist American society in order to value one's black humanity. Double consciousness may also be described by interaction with the veil as a projector screen; the veil lowers over the body of black people to serve as a movie screen allowing only the projected image from the collective white imagination to be seen, while actual black humanity is hidden behind the veil. Black people know real black humanity within or behind the veil, in addition to the contrived white image upon it. In 1926, Du Bois argued that the criteria of Negro art turns black artists into "apostles of beauty," which is to say, apostles of truth and right, which turns the artistic representations by black artists into justice work in the service of acknowledging real black humanity.[10] The apostle of beauty is bound by the claims of justice to tell what they know about real black people, offering a humanizing representation of black life in distinction from the dehumanizing depictions upon the veil that originate in the Dreams of white people.

The two un-reconciled strivings that Du Bois identifies represent part of the struggle at the heart of black life in the United States: to unravel the tension caused by the intrapersonal strivings of double consciousness by lifting the veil, reconciling the two selves, and disclosing the souls of black folk. Beasts do not have souls, but human beings do. The white imagination of the Negro is negative out-group distortion, depicting black people as soul-less to establish black sub-humanity and to stabilize the notion of the "human being" as a reference for whites only. The veil and double consciousness are targets of the struggle to de-stabilize the white imagination as normative for black people.

And although one of the destructive social effects of white supremacy is the distortion of real black life, those destructive effects are not reserved for blacks only. People who believe they are white are also disfigured by it. In a subsequent essay published in 1920 titled, "The Souls of White Folk," Du Bois argues that whiteness distorts the humanity of white people and is responsible for mass destruction on a global scale. If racism reconfigures black people as sub-human, it also trains white people to see whiteness

10. W. E. B. Du Bois, "The Criteria of Negro Art," *The Crisis* 32 (1926).

as divinity. In the years post–World War I, Du Bois identified racism as the operative ideology that shaped white people to see whiteness as, "the ownership of the earth forever and ever, Amen!"[11] The effect of this soul-distorting imagination is to calibrate deity by a template of whiteness, linking white people to God, and giving whites a place of perpetual ascendancy on earth, "as it is in heaven." Du Bois claims that during the pre–World War I modern colonial period, Western European empires marshaled this ideology to arrange their empires as the domains of sovereign demi-gods, each with his own claims to pieces of colonized earth and rights to all of the resources in their colonial territories, including the bodies within it, all the while lusting for more. It was the lustful claims of white sovereign demi-gods emerging from the neocolonialism of the Scramble for Africa that brought the world into a cataclysm of death and destruction in World War I.[12]

Racism is the stabilizing ideology of human difference for neocolonialism to normalize white supremacy in the colonial relationship between Europeans and Africans, categorizing them according to a contrived hierarchy of beings. White supremacy served as a bio-political organizing scheme, justified by religious convictions that saw God as the most high and white men as the only ones who are made in his image and burdened with the task of ruling the world.

In his essay titled "Everyone's Protest Novel," Baldwin argued that the criteria that inform our social understanding of human beings bind everyone to the same reality, "the oppressed and the oppressor are bound together within the same society; they both accept the same criteria, they share the same beliefs, they both alike depend on the same reality."[13] Hence core beliefs about anthropology operate on both sides of the color line whether or not one embraces religious claims. Coates's repeated references to people who believe they are white invokes the history of race as a system of belief. It gestures towards the religious status of whiteness that gives theological cogency to its practice of hegemony over the label human being.

11. W. E. B. Du Bois, *Darkwater: Voices from within the Veil* (Mineola, NY: Dover), 18.

12. Du Bois, *Darkwater*, 17–29.

13. Baldwin, "Everybody's Protest Novel," in *James Baldwin: Collected Essays,* edited byToni Morrison. (New York: Library of America, 1998), 17.

BLACKNESS BEYOND THE STRUGGLE

Beliefs drive our core convictions. Beliefs inform how we see the world, and they shape our understanding of what it means to be human. If we situate our self-understanding as black people in the United States only in the struggle against white supremacy, we unwittingly partner with the ideological forces that distort our understanding of ourselves as human by positioning our epistemology within white supremacy.

For this reason, Coates's offering of "only the struggle" to his son is problematic. To know black life one must not only understand the struggle, one must look beyond the struggle. That is what writers like Zora Neale Hurston did. Hurston was less concerned with the struggle of black existence in opposition to white supremacy, and more concerned with the beauty and complexity of black life in the world, as it is in itself. As Hurston indicates, one should not ignore the struggle, but to know black humanity requires that one also come to know black life that is not tethered to the efforts of white people to secure a white world.

Eboni Marshall Turman makes this argument in her book *Towards a Womanist Ethic of Incarnation: Black Bodies, The Black Church, and the Council of Chalcedon.*[14] She argues that black people are mistaken when we assume that the content that makes for self-awareness comes to us primarily from the outside, passing through the filtering process of white supremacy before becoming a black possession. In that case, black self-knowledge is dependent upon an epistemological captivity to the treatment of black bodies in a white racist world. Understanding black identity in that way, primarily as reaction to white supremacy, tethers blackness to racism, and serves merely to reproduce the ignobility of supremacy and domination within black communities.

There is more to black identity than the struggle against the history of white supremacy. That's not to say that the centuries of struggle are not formative for black people, culture, and communal understanding. The struggle is real, but there is also life undefined by struggle against white supremacy, what Marshall Turman describes as a "Just isness" that describes the inherent value to all humanity, in addition to the historically discursive interaction between black people and white supremacy. It is the claim that

---

14. Eboni Marshall Turman, *Toward a Womanist Ethic of Incarnation: Black Bodies, the Black Church, and the Council of Chalcedon* (New York: Palgrave MacMillan, 2013).

we, too, are people who are made in love, and share the image of God, not only the scars of the struggle.

WHITE SUPREMACY AS A SYSTEM OF BELIEF

The struggle is against a foe that is as insidious as it is malicious. It is a hierarchy of human worth that includes practices of financial exploitation that are justified by the claims of common interests between poor and wealthy whites, by white supremacy. W. E. B. Du Bois argued that, rather than joining with blacks, with whom poor whites shared concrete economic survival interests, white supremacy pays intangible wages to the poor. It serves as ideological funding for capitalism and it scuttles democracy; white supremacy serves as another form of compensation for poor whites who historically prefer to eke out an existence with low wages rather than protest their economic exploitation alongside black people.[15] Hence, the white working class have not been passive recipients of crafty ideology fashioned by elites to divide and conquer the poor; they too have been co-conspirators to their own financial detriment, embracing and contributing to a nefarious and insidious anthropology. Their contribution has been self-sacrificial.

White supremacy is a type of belief system that encourages sacrifice. People of color are placed on the altar to legitimize white supremacy as a good worth striving for. It gives to its adherents sacred convictions to guide core concepts like human nature, morality, beauty, decency, intelligence, an understanding of Jesus, and of the mission of the church. To address people who believe they are white is also to interact with devotees of a social-political ideology that functions as a religion. Yet, one does not need to be white to be a devotee of whiteness; whiteness has its converts of color who are also persuaded by it as a financially incentivized anthropology, to embrace its hierarchy of human worth.

BLACK RELIGION AND THE STRUGGLE

To omit interaction with black religiosity is to omit core formative content that has sustained black people in the midst of the hierarchy of human worth. Beliefs that sustained black life in white America are more than what

---

15. David R. Roediger, *The Wages of Whiteness : Race and the Making of the American Working Class* (London: Verso, 2007).

one finds inside of a church. They also sustain black political and social activism that demands acknowledgement of black humanity by disentangling the false connection made between whiteness and divinity. As a confession of faith, black religiosity informs a different Christian moral life than its white counterpart, as it must respond to different sets of circumstances. Major Jones described this phenomenon by reference to the ethical question "what ought I to do?" to make his claims about Christian ethics for black theology. For Christians, the question "what ought I to do?" gestures towards Luke's gospel and the moment when a legal authority asked Jesus the same question, "what must I do to inherit eternal life" (Luke 10:25). As Jones describes, one's situation in society's hierarchy of human worth will determine the answer to that question:

> If the answer to the same moral questions, derived from the same set of ethical, principles, models, or values, are to be altered by what one has become or what he is as a person [within the hierarchy of human worth], then to be black in pro-white America is, perhaps, to be ethical in a quite different sense. It is to act ethically in a different way . . . Is the ethical mandate for the black and white Christian the same?[16]

The criterion that structures the collective understanding of human being informs the social and political value of our bodies. The resulting encounter between blacks and whites in the United States betrays the lie that white Christianity has something concrete to offer society beyond the Dreams it gives to whites of idealized humanity for idealized community. As intellectuals like Du Bois and Major Jones argue, white Christianity often manifests as a disembodied emphasis on confession and creed over social interaction. But, a black faith expression highlights social interaction as the point of departure for recognizing faithful Christian living.

Charles Long's description of theologies of the opaque may be helpful at this point. Opacity in this mode is regarded differently than the opaque veil that Du Bois refers to in light of the white racial imagination. Here, opaque is a positive contrast to transparent. People of color are rendered transparent within the white racial hierarchy, which organizes humanity according to the template of the normalized white masculine body, and biological markers like skin color become physical indicators of intangible character qualities and social worth. Long describes the crucifixion as a

16. Major J. Jones, *Christian Ethics for Black Theology* (Nashville: Abingdon, 1974), 16.

graphic illustration of transparency. Accordingly, on the cross, Jesus became transparent; the suffering body is rendered invisible as worshippers look past the body towards an abstract of God. Theologians of opacity will not allow this suffering body to be ignored, which is the historical treatment it receives within the hegemonic anthropologies associated with white Christianity. What is demanded in this case is that the lives of people relegated to invisibility and non-being, the bodies who suffer in plain view of society, become apparent and that their suffering is morally unaccounted for. Opacity is an epistemological arrangement that recalibrates the location of knowing from the abstract towards the concrete where the question "what ought I to do," is derived from social encounters.[17]

CONCLUSION

Finally, Although Coates's book is a letter shared between a black father and son, it is important to acknowledge the way gender is unaccounted for in his descriptions of the Dream, and the struggle. As males, Coates and his son remain privileged in a society that is not only racist, but sexist, classist, and homophobic. To focus on one level of analysis, on race alone, is to ignore the ways that oppression works on multiple levels to render suffering invisible. Coates and his black son may perpetuate someone else's struggle, a struggle that they may choose to ignore, because they are middle-class black men. But if we are to participate in the undoing of hierarchies of human worth, we must pay attention to the way that multiple oppressed identities intersect in the shadows of idealized humanity.

I am grateful for this work from Ta-Nehisi Coates, and for the conversation that it has helped to generate. I am sure that it will continue to fund fruitful dialogue, especially in our current times of struggle. In the end, this struggle and this dialogue must help us to know something real about ourselves, beyond the abstract ideologies that seek to define us, towards the concrete where we may actually know ourselves, and one another. White people as well as black people struggle to understand what we are actually dealing with in regards to race, but it is also important to know who we are, who we really are, in addition to what white people make of the world, in their dreams.

17. Charles H. Long, *Significations: Signs, Symbols, and Images in the Interpretation of Religion* (Aurora, CO: Davies Group, 1999).

7

HOPE'S VAGARIES

How Ta-Nehisi Coates and Vincent Harding Convinced
Me That Hope Is Not the Only Option

— TOBIN MILLER SHEARER[1] —

In preparation for a sermon in the late 1990s, I asked one hundred people in the course of one month, "What gives you hope?" Respondents from across the political spectrum—elected officials, former teachers, high school friends, and famous writers—offered insight. Yet one of the most striking encounters took place while pulling my sons—then two and four years old—in a wagon through the inner-city section of Lancaster City, Pennsylvania; as we crested the hill at the intersection of S. Ann and King Streets where Champ's Barbershop attracted a faithful clientele, a group of African-American young men stood chatting on the sidewalk. I walked up to them, introduced myself, and asked, "What gives you hope?" In response, they looked baffled, apparently uncertain of what to make of this skinny white man and his two white sons. An awkward silence settled on us. I thanked them for their time and continued on my way.

1. The author wishes to thank the following interlocutors for their insightful engagement with his work: Courtney Arntzen, Victoria Cech, Julie and Steve Edwards, Felipe Hinojosa, Linda Karell, and Ashby Kinch.

But the interaction troubled me. On the one hand, my failure to evoke a response made perfect sense. The abrupt nature of my question, the public venue of our encounter, and the history of white interlopers in our neighborhood set up distrust between us. Nonetheless, I could not stop wondering what they would have said had they answered. Would they have dismissed the very warrant of the question—that hope mattered from the onset? Would they have decried the question as irrelevant? Or would they have proclaimed a deep and abiding hope far more robust than my own?

The writing of Ta-Nehisi Coates along with civil rights activist, scholar, and sage Vincent Harding prompted me to consider again my question about hope and the young men's response to it. In particular, I began to pursue a question that emerged from the religious grounding of my inquiry and the racial subtext of that chance meeting on Ann and King Streets: "How does one's posture toward hope shape one's stance against racism?" My answer emerges from a comparison of the writing of an avowed atheist—Coates—with that of a professing Christian—Harding—and turns on hope's vagaries. Finding little utility in hope, Coates emphasizes how often history's harsh realities render it false. Harding finds within that same history a struggle-born, blood-thick hope grounded in the promise of the future. But both authors' stance against racism shows that hope—regardless of its basis—is not the only option. Given hope's vagaries, other motivating forces sometimes prove more apposite. Although this conclusion leaves me both more enamored of and frustrated with the role of hope in history, I have also come to better understand the young men's silence as they stood on the sidewalk outside Champ's barbershop.

The comparison of the two men begins with their religious backgrounds. Born in 1931, Harding grew up attending a small black Seventh-Day Adventist congregation in Harlem with his mother. Born in 1975, Coates grew up reading Black Panther books in Baltimore with his father. After earning degrees in history and journalism, Harding went on to study the history of Christianity at the University of Chicago and pastor both Adventist and Mennonite congregations before serving in Atlanta alongside Martin Luther and Coretta Scott King. Coates attended Howard University for a time before pursuing a full-time career as a journalist and eventually asserting his atheism.

Both writers came to achieve significant writing success. Harding penned King's anti-Vietnam War speech in 1967 and served as the King Center's first director before eventually garnering a post at Iliff School of

Theology in Denver in 1981, the same year that he published his highly regarded black history, *There Is a River.*[2] He continued to teach from his position as Professor of Religion and Social Change at Iliff, promote connections between activists and academics, and speak on spiritual themes through to his death in 2014. As readers of this volume are already aware, Coates found work as a writer at *The Atlantic* beginning in 2008 where he gained a wide audience, penned important essays on reparations, mass incarceration, and public schools among many other topics, and eventually released his memoir *Between the World and Me*. He continues to write for *The Atlantic* while pursuing other creative projects, most notably his *Black Panther* series for Marvel Comics.

As these brief biographical reviews suggest, Harding and Coates share a host of similarities. Both offer eloquent, passionate, and sophisticated insight into the history and contemporary realities of race, racism, and the American project. Both are highly committed to supporting the black community. Both offer challenges to the racial status quo, and perhaps most importantly, both share a love of the written word and the crafting of it.[3] Harding captures what is their most important contribution—the telling of stories. He writes, "And I suggest that we are already living inside our own stories, as if we were storied into being. In the same way that food and water are essential to our survival, stories are also essential. Gathering together to tell stories is absolutely necessary for every human society."[4] That is the work to which they are fundamentally committed.

But perhaps most strikingly, both criticize the practice of religion in general and Christianity in particular. Note Harding's 1967 comparison of the work of revolutionary Marxists to practicing Christians. "They [the revolutionaries]," Harding writes, "appear to be more ready to die for their convictions than many Christians."[5] He is far less patient with those who

2. Tobin Miller Shearer, "A Prophet Pushed Out: Vincent Harding and the Mennonites," *Mennonite Life* 69 (2015), https://ml.bethelks.edu/issue/vol-69/article/a-prophet-pushed-out-vincent-harding-and-the-menno/.

3. To facilitate ease of prose, I have chosen to write about the two men in the present tense except when making specific historical references to one or the other's body of work. Dr. Harding's voice is still very much alive and present with us through his written work.

4. Vincent Harding and Daisaku Ikeda, *America Will Be!: Conversations on Hope, Freedom, and Democracy* (Cambridge, MA: Dialogue Path, 2013), 27.

5. Vincent Harding, "The Peace Witness and Revolutionary Movements," *Mennonite Life* 22, no. 4 (1967): 161–65.

claimed religious faith but did not act upon it than he is with those who made no such claims of faith from the start. In defense of the Black Power movement Harding opines, "It may be that America must now stand under profound and damning judgment for having turned the redeeming lover of all men into a white, middle-class burner of children and destroyer of the revolutions of the oppressed."[6]

Coates, as already noted, writes as an avowed atheist. His criticism starts from his bedrock acceptance of "the chaos of history and the fact of my total end" without any appeal to what he calls "magic."[7] He views religion as a force that offers comfort where none should be provided, an improper crutch that only serves to delay healing, a false and debilitating promise of better things to come. As an example, he notes that religion does nothing but pacify the prison population of Louisiana's notorious Angola prison and thereby perpetuates "a great human-rights disaster."[8]

That shared criticism of religion also connects with their most fundamental difference. Harding sees possibility and promise in the practice of religion; Coates does not. In this they follow the expectations of their respective religious identities even while both exhibiting a fierce commitment to intellectual integrity.

Harding frequently highlights faith communities who live out their convictions. Professing belief in the Holy Spirit's power to compel Christians "beyond all the limits of physical, intellectual, and spiritual safety that we know now" to bring joy to "broken victims" and elation to the "humiliated," Harding celebrates Christians' self-sacrificial actions.[9] Harding praises the black church leaders who stood "firm on the front lines against the moral evil of segregation."[10] He lifts up the example of Mennonites

6. Gayraud S. Wilmore and James H. Cone, *Black Theology: A Documentary History,* 1966–1979 (Maryknoll, NY : Orbis, 1979), 41.

7. Ta-Nehisi Coates, *Between the World and Me* (New York: Spiegel & Grau, 2015), 12.

8. Ta-Nehisi Coates and Jeffrey Goldberg, "So What's the Solution to Mass Incarceration? Goldberg V. Coates," *The Atlantic,* http://www.theatlantic.com/notes/all/2015/09/whats-the-solution-to-mass-incarceration/405757/#note-406078.

9. Harding, "Revolutionary Movements," 165.

10. Harding, "Vincent Harding: A Black Historian," in *Peace-Makers: Christian Voices from the New Abolitionist Movement,* ed. Jim Wallis (San Francisco: Harper and Row, 1983), 85–97; Harding, "We the People: The Long Journey toward a More Perfect Union," in *The Eyes on the Prize Civil Rights Reader: Documents, Speeches, and Firsthand Accounts from the Black Freedom Struggle, 1954–1990,* ed. Clayborne Carson, et al. (New York: Penguin Books, 1991), 1–34, at 32–33.

like white pastor Titus Bender who risked social opprobrium and physical retaliation by greeting Vincent and Rosemarie with the traditional Mennonite Holy Kiss in public.[11] And he lauds the ministry of small urban religious communities who "dance[d] their praise on the basketball court, . . . create[d] home for each other and the folks around them . . ., [and] brave[d] the occasional stray bullets" to create church amid poverty and neglect.[12] Not limiting his positive assessment of religion just to Christianity, Harding also praises members of the Hindu, Jewish, and Islamic communities for their prophetic witness and the "essential unity between democratic politics and soulful religion."[13]

Harding also extends his praise to more controversial figures. He notes that Nat Turner, the infamous leader of a bloody slave revolt in Virginia in 1831, led his rebellion from a "religious center" of belief "that he was the anointed one of God" to bring freedom to his people.[14] In the same way, Harding emphasizes the religious connections of Gullah Jack in Denmark Vesey's failed 1822 rebellion in Charleston, South Carolina, and the bedrock faith of Underground Railroad leader Harriet Tubman.[15] For Harding, religious conviction does not distract from struggle; it is the ground from which it springs.

Yet his belief in religion's efficacy does not mitigate his intellectual exploration of its internal contradictions. Harding recognizes, for example, that those who sang spirituals did so for many reasons. Some sang to escape earthly bounds and make "the experiences of their surroundings fade in importance," while others found "a new determination to struggle, build,

---

11. Rachel E. Harding, "Biography, Democracy, and Spirit: An Interview with Vincent Harding," *Callaloo* 20, no. 3 (1998): 682–98, at 696; Vincent Harding and Joanna Shenk, "Anabaptist Formation: An Interview with Vincent Harding," in *Widening the Circle: Experiments in Christian Discipleship*, ed. Joanna Shenk (Harrisonburg, VA: Herald Press, 2011), 23–34, at 28–29.

12. Vincent Harding, *Is America Possible?: A Letter to My Young Companion on the Journey of Hope* (Kalamazoo, MI: Fetzer Institute, 2007), 19.

13. Harding, *Hope and History: Why We Must Share the Story of the Movement* (Maryknoll, New York: Orbis, 1990, 2009), 9; Harding, "We the People," 32–33.

14. Harding, "You've Taken My Nat and Gone," in *William Styron's Nat Turner: Ten Black Writers Respond*, ed. John Henrik Clarke (Boston: Beacon, 1968), 23–33, at 28; Harding, "Religion and Resistance among Antebellum Slaves," in *African-American Religion: Interpretive Essays in History and Culture*, ed. Timothy E. Fulop and Albert J. Raboteau (New York: Routledge, 1997), 108–30, at 117.

15. Harding, "Religion and Resistance," 108–30.

and resist" oppression while yet on earth.[16] Harding referred to this duality as a "doubleness" that, in the case of slavery, "often stormed beyond submissiveness to defiance."[17] In his view, the very ones who found solace in religious practice might also find cause for revolution.

Coates gives the practice of religion far less credit. In his worldview, there is only the body. God has no role to play. With an uncommonly precise existential clarity Coates avows, "I believe that when they shatter the body they shatter everything, and . . . all of us—Christians, Muslims, atheists—lived in the sphere of this truth" (113–4). This conviction, every bit as deep as that of Harding's in the presence of the divine, turns him away from the possibility of forgiveness for those who destroy the body because "our bodies are our selves, . . . my soul is the voltage conducted through neurons and nerves, and . . . my spirit is my flesh."[18] Coates adds that he cannot join in the piety of prayer because he believes "that the void would not answer back."[19]

Rather than religion, Coates draws on epistemology. For him, it is not knowledge of the divine that holds promise for sustenance in the midst of struggle but rather knowledge of the world's fragility. An understanding of "how fragile everything . . . really is" allows a kind of "love power" to sustain the black community—or at least specific members of it.[20] Here Coates expresses an idea similar to the Buddhist concept of impermanence, the insight that all things are subject to dissolution.[21] That said, Coates's articulation stands on its own independent of any religious tradition. He promotes knowledge of fragility rather than belief and practice built around it.

Given such disparate views on the saliency of religion, Coates and Harding could be expected to take fundamentally different approaches to critiquing racism and whiteness. At first glance, however, there seems to be little variation. To begin, both contend that white identity is rooted in violence and power. Coates notes that a white collective developed not through "wine tastings and ice cream socials" but "through the pillaging of life, liberty, labor and land; through the flaying of backs; the chaining of

16. Harding, "Religion and Resistance," 126.

17. Harding, "Religion and Resistance," 110.

18. Harding, "Religion and Resistance," 79.

19. Harding, "Religion and Resistance," 79.

20. Harding, "Religion and Resistance," 149.

21. James C. Livingston, *Anatomy of the Sacred: An Introduction to Religion* (New York: Macmillan, 1989), 236.

limbs; . . . the rape of mothers; the sale of children" (8). With equal stark-ness, Harding declares that white Mennonites "clearly control the power, subtle power, like the power of Mennonite prestige, the power of middle-class respectability, the power of whiteness."[22]

And this is where hope enters in.

The difference between Coates's atheistic and Harding's confessional approach to critiquing whiteness is grounded in the presence or absence of hope. In an essay entitled "Hope and the Artist," Coates finds hope to be an impediment to intellectual inquiry and discourse. "[H]ope for hope's sake, hope as tautology, hope because hope, hope because 'I said so,'" he avers, "is the enemy of intelligence."[23] In another essay exploring history's hard truths, he adds "a writer wedded to 'hope' is ultimately divorced from 'truth.' Two creeds can't occupy the same place at the same time."[24] So trenchant is his critique of hope that Coates goes on to assert, "[W]riters who commit themselves to only writing hopeful things, are committing themselves to the ahistorical, to the mythical, to the hagiography of humanity itself."[25]

Even when Coates dabbles in hope, he does so at a remove. At the conclusion of *Between the World and Me*, Coates advises his son Samori, "Do not struggle for the Dreamers. Hope for them." Yet his advice to hope for the Dreamers appears suspect as he—the declared atheist—then writes, "Pray for them, if you are so moved" (151). More irony and rhetorical flour-ish than sage counsel, this dabbling in hope makes Coates's deep distrust evident; he knows how often hope has been used to deny history's horror and calls out the danger that he sees.

By contrast, Harding is immersed in hope. And it is the presence of that hope that intensifies his critique of whiteness. In his writing, Harding expects white Christians to be better than those around them, to act in more just ways than those who have not been given the promise of the eschaton. He has hope that white people will not conform to the ways of whiteness. And when that hope is betrayed, the bitterness is palpable.

That said, Harding's hope is no saccharine artifice. Harding writes with a particular eloquence when describing it. "Somewhere," he expounded in

22. Harding, "Revolutionary Movements," 164.

23. Ta-Nehisi Coates, "Hope and the Artist," *The Atlantic*, http://www.theatlantic.com/entertainment/archive/2015/11/hope-and-the-artist/417348/.

24. Ta-Nehisi Coates, "Hope and the Historian," *The Atlantic*, http://www.theatlantic.com/politics/archive/2015/12/hope-and-the-historian/419961/.

25. Coates, "Hope and the Historian."

1990, "at the heart of this spinning globe there is a fascinating common ground on which we and our students may stand to shape past and present into a vector of hope and responsibility."[26] But, closer to the end of this life, he wrote perhaps his most eloquent and clear-eyed assessment of hope when he distinguished between an "easy, placid, feel-good optimism" and a "rugged, blood-stained hope" born of the:

> dark-womb beauty . . . of struggles for the creative transformation of "ordinary" women, men, and children who refused to give up their extraordinary dreams of new beginnings in Alabama, Mississippi, Soweto, Georgia, Oakland, Prague, Greensboro, Beijing, Chicago, Philadelphia, Berlin, Detroit—in every place else where humans live to nurture and embody their dreams.[27]

The sincerity and ubiquity of that hope, the profound centrality of it to the Christian project of belief and assertion of revealed truth, thus sets up moments of devastation that Coates avoids because he carries no such expectation that racism will be overcome. For Coates, white supremacy is the bedrock foundation of a racist state; it will always be present. He does not acknowledge the possibility of a redeemed future where all such forms of oppression will be overcome. At best, he concedes that white supremacy could diminish or change form even as he unequivocally proclaims, "[I]t will always be with us in some form."[28] And because he has no hope that racism will disappear, he has no hope to lose. He does not despair. By contrast, throughout Harding's writing, especially during the late 1950s through the early 1970s when he was closely aligned with the white Mennonite faith community, a note of deep disappointment bordering on despair recurs. That despairing tone permeates his 1967 call to white Mennonites to become involved in revolutionary efforts to overturn racism and colonialism. He asks, "Are we now the lame, paralyzed because of fear, swaying under the weight of dignity, captured by the power of our possessions? Where are the saints?"[29]

Hope also forms the two writers' assessment of nonviolence. Without an eschatological hope to shape his analysis, Coates acknowledges that "violence sometimes works," using the example of the Civil War as exhibit

26. Harding, *Hope and History*, 4.

27. Harding, *Is America Possible?*, 3.

28. Coates, "Hope and the Historian."

29. Vincent Harding, "The Beggars Are Rising . . . Where Are the Saints?," *Mennonite Life* 22, no. 4 (1967): 152–53.

number one.[30] He likewise observes that blacks are expected to honor only nonviolent heroes while whites are allowed more violent role models (32). In this he is correct. The national historical narrative celebrates many violent white heroes including the original tea party organizers, George Washington, and Daniel Boone. Figures like Nat Turner, Denmark Vesey, Gabriel Prosser, and other black proponents of violence receive little to no attention. At the same time, Coates is not without praise for Martin Luther King Jr.'s "annoying habit of preaching nonviolence, whether it was convenient or not."[31] He also cautions against "lionizing killing" by noting "even if nonviolence isn't always the answer, King reminds us to work for a world where it is."[32] And so, within Coates's body of work we see a nuanced and historically grounded assessment of the benefits and limitations of both violence and nonviolence.

Harding's assessment of the relative merits of violence and non-violence begins with a similarly balanced evaluation. Like Coates, he, too, recognizes the violence at the root of American society, noting that it is "built into the American grain."[33] Harding also acknowledges the power and determination present within slave rebellions and other violent acts of resistance in African-American history. For example, he praises how "enslaved Africans" in Stono, South Carolina, took up arms in 1739 in a bid to repossess "their own identity . . . as soldiers of liberty."[34] Although unsuccessful, the struggle for freedom serves for Harding as another example of "[t]his black struggle for freedom, this insistent Black movement towards justice, the centuries-long black search for a new America . . . this . . . Other American Revolution."[35] Yet, having lauded such acts of organized violence, Harding returns repeatedly to the power of nonviolence, grounded as it is in a hope for a better world. Like Coates, he, too, valorizes King noting that "Martin was guided in every situation by a spirit of nonviolence, and he refused to let fear of infiltrators dominate his thinking."[36]

30. Ta-Nehisi Coates, "Killing Dylann Roof," *The Atlantic*, May 26, 2016.

31. Coates, "Killing Dylann Roof."

32. Coates, "Killing Dylann Roof."

33. Vincent Harding, "Where Have All the Lovers Gone?," *Mennonite Life*, January 1967, 11.

34. Harding, *The Other American Revolution* (Los Angeles: University of California, 1980), 13.

35. Harding, *Other American Revolution*, xv.

36. Harding and Ikeda, *America Will Be!*, 73.

But what distinguishes Harding's approach from Coates's is that Harding is willing to commit himself to an ethic of nonviolence and promote it unequivocally. In his moving and provocative tribute, *Martin Luther King: The Inconvenient Hero*, Harding calls for a revolution grounded in King's hope-filled vision of a "new life through nonviolence, noncooperation, massive civil disobedience, and love."[37] Rather than just describe that vision, Harding urges his readers to join that revolution by asking "does our God given humanity leave us with any other authentic choice at this moment in history?"[38]

Here the hope that Harding carries manifests itself as more than a creator of false expectations. It appears as more than the impetus of bitter disappointment. The hope at the root of Harding's passion for a better world prods him to take action. To be certain, Coates also calls for action. But Coates does not offer the same focused promotion of the nonviolent ideal. Regardless of how much respect he holds for King, Coates views nonviolence as an effective tactic in some circumstances but not in others.[39] Harding sees in nonviolence the possibility of not only organizing mass action but making another kind of world into a reality, one brought into being by the "blood-stained hope" that he holds so dear.[40]

That distinction between commentator on nonviolence and proponent of it does not extend to other solutions to the problem of racism. Both

37. Vincent Harding, *Martin Luther King, the Inconvenient Hero* (Maryknoll, NY: Orbis, 1996), 79.

38. Harding, *Martin Luther King*, 79.

39. For discussion of violence and non-violence in the civil rights movement and the varying approaches to it, begin with this sampling of the burgeoning literature focused on this very issue: Charles M. Payne, *I've Got the Light of Freedom: The Organizing Tradition and the Mississippi Freedom Struggle* (Berkeley: University of California Press, 1995); Simon Wendt, "The Roots of Black Power?: Armed Resistance and the Radicalization of the Civil Rights Movement," in *The Black Power Movement: Rethinking the Civil Rights-Black Power Era*, ed. Peniel E. Joseph (New York: Routledge, 2006), 145–65; Hasan Kwame Jeffries, *Bloody Lowndes: Civil Rights and Black Power in Alabama's Black Belt* (New York: New York University Press, 2009); Charles E. Cobb Jr., *This Nonviolent Stuff'll Get You Killed: How Guns Made the Civil Rights Movement Possible* (New York: Basic Books, 2014); Tobin Miller Shearer, "Striking at the Sacred: The Violence of Prayer, 1960–1969," *Open Theology* 1 (2015): 126–33; Wesley Hogan, "Freedom Now: Nonviolence in the Southern Freedom Movement, 1960–1964," in *Civil Rights History from the Ground Up*, ed. Emilye Crosby (Athens: University of Georgia Press, 2011), 172–93; Timothy B. Tyson, *Radio Free Dixie: Robert F. Williams and the Roots of Black Power* (Chapel Hill: University of North Carolina Press, 1999).

40. Harding, *Is America Possible?*, 3.

writers speak to and have connections with the movement to institute slavery reparations. While not a direct advocate for James Forman's 1969 "Black Manifesto To the White Christian Church and the Jewish Synagogues in the United States of America and All Other Racist Institutions," Harding's name appeared on the list of black dignitaries slated to give direction to the expenditure of funds garnered from this reparations campaign.[41] Coates wrote a widely disseminated and critically praised call for slavery reparations in which he argues that the payment of reparations would air "family secrets," settle "old ghosts," heal the "American psyche," and banish "white guilt."[42] In their approach to reparations, both men recognize that friendship-based solutions, feel-good paeans to interracial relationships, and photos of black-white embrace will not address the deep-seated issues of white supremacy, power, and privilege at the core of U.S. racism. Instead Coates and Harding call for ending mass incarceration, overhauling drug policies, reforming lending practices, stabilizing voting rights, and funding educational institutions.[43] Harding puts it this way: "Hearts are not relevant to the issue; neither racial affinities nor racial hostilities are rooted there. It is institutions—social, political, and economic institutions—which are the ultimate molders of collective sentiments."[44] Regardless of their respective approaches to hope, both men identify institutions rather than individuals as the necessary locus of change.

Neither Harding nor Coates believe reparations or institutional change sufficient; both reach toward more universal themes. Coates finds his ultimate imperative in "love." As expected, however, his idea of love

41. James Forman, "Black Manifesto to the White Christian Church and the Jewish Synagogues in the United States of America and All Other Racist Institutions," Detroit, Michigan, National Black Economic Development Conference, 1969, 12.

42. Ta-Nehisi Coates, "The Case for Reparations," *The Atlantic*, June 2014, 58.

43. Ta-Nehisi Coates, "The Black Family in the Age of Mass Incarceration," *The Atlantic*, http://www.theatlantic.com/magazine/archive/2015/10/the-black-family-in-the-age-of-mass-incarceration/403246/; Ta-Nehisi Coates, "The Racist Housing Policies That Built Ferguson," *The Atlantic*, October 17, 2014; Ta-Nehisi Coates, "The Littlest Schoolhouse," *The Atlantic*, July/August 2010, http://www.theatlantic.com/magazine/archive/2010/07/the-littlest-schoolhouse/308132/; Vincent Harding, "Introduction," in *If Your Back's Not Bent: The Role of the Citizenship Education Program in the Civil Rights Movement* (New York: Atria, 2012), xv–xxi; Harding, "Awakenings (1954–1956)," in *The Eyes on the Prize Civil Rights Reader: Documents, Speeches, and Firsthand Accounts from the Black Freedom Struggle, 1954–1990*, ed. Clayborne Carson et al. (New York: Penguin, 1991), 35–37.

44. Harding, "Where Have All," 9.

holds no space for saccharine nostalgia, fawning sentimentality, or rose-scented romance. Rather, Coates allows for "softness" but centers on love as "an act of heroism" given freely, often unexpectedly, and rooted in protection of and care for the black body (61). That love stems from his grounding in "people," his people, the black community that has sustained, nurtured, and elicited the "broad love" that allows him to express a "specific love" for his son.[45] The love shows up for Coates not only in relationships and family connections but also in poetry and art, of both the classical and pop culture variety.[46]

For Harding, hope and democracy prove most inspiring. In the struggle for democracy he finds not only a "disciplined compassion and vision" but also universal "lessons that were meant for us all" about the ultimate imperatives of truth, justice and—again—hope.[47] In the fight for a "democratic America," Harding celebrates "new settings that do not yet exist" while also affirming the "great gifts and resources that constantly surprise the world" in the midst of struggle.[48] But Harding is at his most ebullient when he writes of youth. It is the promise of "the powerful inner resources" of young people that fosters a network of "hope across the globe."[49] The youth who bring "their best selves, their best strength, their most powerful visions" will build a more democratic society and a "more just and peaceable world people."[50]

These broad themes set the stage for a final declaration of the unity within these two authors' work because, even though hope sets them apart, it also brings them together. St. Augustine wrote of hope already in the late fourth and early fifth centuries when he observed, "Hope has two beautiful daughters, anger and courage; anger at the way things are, and courage to work to make things other than they are."[51] The eschatological hope that grounds Harding's writing and makes Coates so uncomfortable

45. Harding, "Where Have All," 88.

46. Coates, "Mass Incarceration and the Problem of Language," *The Atlantic*, http://www.theatlantic.com/notes/all/2015/09/debating-mass-incarceration/405694/#note-405511; Coates, "Hope and the Artist."

47. Harding, *Hope and History*, 8.

48. Harding, "Introduction," xxi.

49. Harding, *Hope and History*, 62.

50. Harding, *Hope and History*, 62.

51. Emilie Maureen Townes, ed., *Embracing the Spirit: Womanist Perspectives on Hope, Salvation, and Transformation*, Bishop Henry Mcneal Turner/Sojourner Truth Series in Black Religion 13 (Maryknoll, NY: Orbis, 1997), 12.

nonetheless carries the marks of some of the best of what each author has to offer. Whether or not they stand on the foundation of hope, both writers articulate their anger at the past, persistent, and present practice of racism; both writers evince unfaltering courage in their declamations about the same. In so doing, they join a long list of black leaders from Marcus Garvey to Ida B. Wells and from Ella Baker to Malcolm X who have done likewise.

Hope thus makes apparent that, confessional differences aside, both Coates and Harding want the same thing and go about their struggles in a similar way. Armed with the pen, they move into places of racial struggle—whether Chicago, Cleveland, DC, or Detroit—and lift up the examples that they find there. For Coates it is enough to simply point to the sign of struggle and say, "See this. Look at it. Don't turn away for the struggle you are witnessing. Observe. Note. Remember." For Coates the struggle is the meaning itself; there is no divine presence to imbue it with eschatological import. For Harding, the struggle is sustained by and symbolic of a greater Power that works through and is present in human action; but that Power does not remove or take away the struggle simply by request. Harding calls for and reminds us of the "canopy of hope" that sustained notions of the "beloved community" as articulated by King during the 1960s.[52] Coates celebrates the poetry of the streets and power of enlightenment.[53] Yet those distinct calls do not contradict or result in different strategies. In addition to anger and courage, Coates and Harding also share a belief in the power of the written word, the saliency of rational argumentation, and the importance of history. They realistically assess the possibility of change and do not engage in wishful thinking.

One could ask, "Who in the end offers the more powerful and effective message? Which author will ultimately hold the greatest sway?" A simplistic response might contend that, despite the cogent, concise, and incisive commentary offered by Coates, Harding has the potential to sway the largest audiences. Both authors craft deft and convincing pose, but only Harding offers a modicum of hope to his readers.

But that is too simple of an answer, really. The work of both men is far too complex and subtle for a simple gradation of effect. Rather, the question that proves more interesting and ultimately more revealing is what do

52. Krista Tippett, *Becoming Wise: An Inquiry into the Mystery and Art of Living* (New York: Penguin, 2016), 157.

53. Coates, "Hope and the Artist"; Coates, "Mass Incarceration and the Problem of Language."

their respective bodies of work tell us about hope itself? Harding ultimately shows us that hope has been most foundational and sustaining when it is tempered in struggle, honed by history, and tested through time. Although he does not—to my knowledge—say so himself, his writing suggests that hope, regardless of the historical moment, is only worth having if it is connected to organized resistance in situations of oppression. Or, to push the point, he suggests that hope and oppression are intrinsically linked; the former only exists in the presence of the latter.

As much as this is true, as much as hope only exists or is worth having in situations where there is every reason not to have it, then Harding and Coates are in agreement. Coates believes in the permanence of racism, and yet he continues to struggle against it. Harding acknowledges the deep-seated nature of racial oppression, and yet he never stopped resisting the many ways it manifested in the world around him. Both authors find a way to move forward, a way to find meaning in the face of an overwhelming system of oppression. Whether they call it hope is, in the end, less important than that they have found a way to not give in to despair.

In this regard, Coates's writing resonates with that of French philosopher Albert Camus when he wrote as part of the French resistance to Nazi occupation. Camus articulated the paradox of the philosophy of the Absurd in which life has no meaning and yet one chooses to strive to give it meaning despite one's belief that it has none. In the same way, Coates asserts that African Americans have no future chance of escaping the social and institutional forces of racism, and yet the black community should choose to strive to overcome racism despite the conviction that the struggle is ultimately futile. For Camus and Coates, it is the struggle that counts, that offers meaning, that allows one to get up in the morning and enter a new day.[54]

Coates is not the only writer to hold such truths in tension. African-American law professor and critical race theorist Derrick Bell also contends that the forces of racism in America are so profound as to be insurmountable.[55] He argues that the only times black Americans have made steps toward racial equality have been when their interests coincided with the

54. Thanks to my friend Stephan Edwards for first making this comparison between Coates and Camus while we ate freeze-dried dinners in the Pintler Wilderness area of Montana.

55. John Torpey, "Paying for the Past?: The Movement for Reparations for African-Americans," *Journal of Human Rights* 3, no. 2 (2004): 171–87, at 175.

interests of powerful whites.[56] The example of Cold War politicians who sided with black Civil Rights activists in order to counter Communist propaganda makes the point. And yet, Bell, too, found meaning and purpose in teaching his law students to resist the racism of the legal system despite the fact that he ultimately believed they had little if any chance of proving successful.

The choice offered by Harding and Coates in the end is not *whether* one will be hopeful or find hope fundamentally suspect. The choice they point to is *what one will draw upon* to resist a system of overwhelming racism. Harding finds his source of strength and sustenance in a robust, battle-born, and unrelenting confessional hope. Coates finds his source of strength in a gritty, focused, and determined commitment to the struggle. From both of them we learn models of sustaining and maintaining strength in the face of overwhelming odds. Whether an articulation of hope is part of the rooting of that struggle seems far less important than that they both have found a way to continue resisting oppression and pass that determination, persistence, and commitment on to others.

I will never know if the young men outside Champ's barbershop would have responded to me if they had encountered the writing of Coates or Harding. But knowing now that hope is only one of many motivations to resist racism, I understand the young men's silence better. In essence, their choice to keep quiet speaks all too loudly of hope. That they chose not to respond to my query, one offered by a strange and foreign white man, was at least a partial sign that they could keep their own counsel. They did not need to respond when prompted. To so remain silent in the face of white interrogation has, at other times and places in history, borne harsh consequences. But there, on that corner of Lancaster City, they did not have to speak aloud of hope and so their silence was itself a hopeful thing.

---

56. Charles R. Lawrence, III, "The Id, the Ego, and Equal Protection: Reckoning with Unconscious Racism," in *Critical Race Theory: The Key Writings That Formed the Movement*, ed. Kimberlé Crenshaw, et al. (New York: New Press, 1995), 235–57, at 254.

8

BETWEEN THE TRAGIC AND THE UNHOPELESS

*Coates, Anti-blackness,
and the Tireless Work of Negativity*

— Joseph Winters —

With all of the praise that Ta-Nehisi Coates's *Between the World and Me* has received, one consistent target of criticism is the lack of hope in Coates's vision. For many commentators, Coates offers a trenchant assessment of black American life and the systemic violence that routinely threatens to possess, and erase, the black body. At the same time, these commentators accuse Coates of rejecting the possibility of a better alternative to the current state. Because he assumes that we are stuck in our predicament, he does not feel obligated to offer a determinate solution to the problems that he diagnoses. Conservative *New York Times* columnist David Brooks exemplifies this sentiment when, in his brief response to *Between the World and Me*, he suggests that Coates offers no hope for change in large part because he renounces the American dream.[1] Michelle Alexander, author

1. See David Brooks, "Listening to Ta-Nehisi Coates While White," *New York Times*, July 17, 2015, https://www.nytimes.com/2015/07/17/opinion/listening-to-ta-nehisi-coates-while-white.html.

of the widely acclaimed *The New Jim Crow*, contends that unlike Coates's literary predecessor, James Baldwin, Coates devalues the importance of believing that the racial order can be transformed. She writes, "Rather than urging his son to awaken to his own power, Coates emphasizes over and over the apparent permanence of racial injustice in America, the foolishness of believing that one person can make a change, and the dangers of believing in the American Dream."[2] For Alexander, those on the progressive side of things must believe in the prospect of justice, a prospect that Coates apparently deems impossible.

While Brooks and Alexander have different political commitments, they share a concern about Coates's pessimism, his relentless negativity that declines a reassuring moment of affirmation. In what follows, I contend that these commentators evade the radical thrust of Coates's argument. For Coates, traditional sites and sources of hope—especially the American dream and the fantasy of progress—simultaneously rely on, and disavow, the (social) death of black bodies. In other words, many of the nation's collective self images and narratives of inspiration work to mollify the tragic quality of America's racial formations. For Coates, a different kind of hope is made possible through melancholy, struggle, and anguished love. This alternative can be described as an un-hopeless drive that finds openings and lines of flight by "tarrying with the negative" and refusing the general demand to be optimistic and conciliatory. To flesh out the relationship between tarrying and creating possibility, I juxtapose Coates and critical theorist Theodor Adorno, an author who has also been accused of pessimism and not offering constructive proposals.[3] I conclude the essay by reading Coates's insights alongside literary historian Saidiya Hartman's description of slavery's "afterlife." While there is significant overlap between Hartman and Coates, I suggest that Hartman offers a more sustained analysis of the relationship between intimacy and violence, or pain and pleasure, within black life.

---

2. Michelle Alexander, "Ta-Nehisi Coates's *Between the World and Me*," *New York Times*, August 17, 2015, http://www.nytimes.com/2015/08/17/books/review/ta-nehisi-coates-between-the-world-and-me.html, Accessed September 25, 2016.

3. On this "failure" in Theodor Adorno's work, see Jürgen Habermas, *The Philosophical Discourse of Modernity*, trans. Frederick Lawrence (Cambridge: MIT Press, 1987), 106–30. I am grateful to my conversations with Jo Nopper on the affinities between Coates and Adorno.

BALDWIN, COATES, AND
THE TRAUMATIC KERNEL OF FANTASY

As Michelle Alexander points out, the style and format of *Between the World and Me* intentionally riffs on James Baldwin's 1963 classic, *The Fire Next Time*.[4] While Baldwin begins his text with a cautionary, but inspiring, letter to his nephew about the hardships and pleasures of black experience, Coates's entire book is written in the form of a letter to his son (a letter that in many ways attempts to rescue his son from various illusions about black existence in America). In addition to the format, Coates adopts Baldwin's critique of American innocence, a disposition that is deeply connected to the assumption that America holds an exceptional status in the world. For Baldwin, the myth of American innocence enables Americans to justify, and readily accept, imperial endeavors to control and dominate populations across the globe. Or to put it differently, this general mythos encodes imperial projects as operations of freedom or as rescue missions, and therefore exonerates the violent quality of these projects. The myth of innocence entices Americans to imagine themselves as exempt from past and present injustices because the widespread *idea* of America, the notion that America stands apart and above as a unique democratic experiment, promises to redeem and make whole the erasures done in the name of this idea and its actualization. This structure of innocence, as Jonathon Kahn points out in his reading of Baldwin, is emblematic of a collective yearning for purity, a desire to be extricated from, and uncontaminated by, the messiness of history and nation-building.[5]

According to Baldwin, this myth of innocence underwrites a certain way of narrating American history, certain ways of remembering, and forgetting, the complexities of the nation's past. As Baldwin describes, the myths that many white Americans cling to suggest "that their ancestors were all freedom-loving heroes, that they were born in the greatest country that the world has ever seen, or that Americans are invincible in battle and

4. To the chagrin of some, Toni Morrison has even labeled Coates our present-day Baldwin.

5. See Jonathon Kahn, "James Baldwin and a Theology of Justice in a Secular Age," in *Race and Secularism in America*, ed. Jonathon Kahn and Vincent Lloyd (New York: Columbia University Press, 2016), 239–56. Kahn is indebted to J. Kameron Carter's contention that modern racial hierarchies are animated by a will to purity and a related logic of self-enclosure. See Carter, *Race: A Theological Account* (New York: Oxford University Press, 2008).

wise in peace, that Americans have always dealt honorably with Mexicans and Indians and all other neighbors or inferiors, that American men are the world's most direct and virile, that American women are pure."[6] There are problems with Baldwin's formulation here, including his assumption that black people are not susceptible to the seductive grip of American-style myths. (This assumption is belied by Michelle Obama's 2016 DNC speech where she proclaims that, contra the Republicans who think that America can be great *again*, America is already the greatest nation on earth.[7]) In addition, we should be vigilant toward the hyperbolic rhetoric used in this passage; to put it differently, we should allow the exaggerated version of American innocence to draw attention to the more subtle ways in which the idea of America operates to generate forgetfulness and deflect responsibility for violence and conflict elsewhere. Even in cases where tension, conflict, and suffering are acknowledged, these signifiers of the negative can be placed in comforting narratives that reassure us of our distance and non-complicity. As Baldwin points out, "Americans have the most remarkable ability to alchemize all bitter truths into an innocuous but piquant confection and to transform their moral contradictions, or public discussion of such contradictions, into a proud decoration, such as are given for heroism on the battlefield."[8] Here Baldwin suggests that many of our discourses and public rituals work to convert contradiction into comfort, tragedy into triumph, bitterness into something palatable. For Baldwin, we cannot understand the persistence of anti-black racism without interrogating how myths and fantasies operate to buffer us from, or inure us to, the violent qualities of racial modernity and human existence.

In a manner that conjures Baldwin, Ta-Nehisi Coates's *Between the World and Me* offers a contemporary interpretation of American innocence and the American dream's incessant "assault on the black body." In the opening section Coates writes, "White America's progress, or rather the progress of those Americans who believe they are white, [is] built on looting and violence."[9] Here Coates introduces a familiar connection between progress and suffering, between the survival, and advancement, of dominant forms

6. James Baldwin, "The Fire Next Time," in *The Price of the Ticket: Collected Fiction, 1948–1985* (New York: St. Martin's, 1985), 377.

7. Michelle Obama, "Democratic National Convention Speech," https://www.youtube.com/watch?v=4ZNWYqDU948.

8. James Baldwin, "Many Thousands Gone," in *The Price of the Ticket*, 65.

9. Ta-Nehisi Coates, *Between the World and Me* (New York: Spiegel and Grau, 2015), 6. Subsequent references will be noted parenthetically in the text.

of life and the violent campaigns against those bodies that stand in the way of progress—or that need to be contained and managed for progress to happen.[10] Among other fraught relationships, Coates is alluding to the association between America's wealth and chattel slavery, the nation's territorial expansion and war, or the general relationship between the accumulation of capital and exploitation/theft. By using the language of "built on," Coates suggests that violence and theft are foundational, constitutive elements of progress. (The home/building that we live in is a broken one.) It is not that the material and psychic benefits of liberal democracy, capital, citizenship, and property ownership have yet to be expanded to include the presently excluded. For Coates these markers of progress rely on the systemic subordination of black bodies, thereby rendering anti-black violence structural and endemic to progress. It is important that Coates uses the term "belief" in this passage when discussing whiteness, suggesting that whiteness is not a natural property or an attribute reducible to skin color; rather it is more like a social imaginary that requires belief and investment in purity, wholeness, and the value of possession. While Coates does not develop this line of thought, we can infer that the project of whiteness—read as belief in, and the practice of, purity and innocence—can conscript subjects and communities that the racial order marks as non-white. What is certain for Coates is that whiteness and progress both produce, and disavow, violence necessary to maintain these projects. These investments promote "the elevation of the belief in being white [which] was not achieved [only] through wine tastings and ice cream socials, but through the pillaging of life, liberty, labor, and land; through the flaying of backs; the chaining of limbs; the strangling of dissidents; the destruction of families; the rape of mothers; the sale of children" (8).

It is also important that Coates juxtaposes lofty ideals or dreams with repeated images of the black body that is always in danger of being dispossessed. In the above passage, for instance, Coates underscores the "flaying of backs" and "the chaining of limbs." The reader is prompted to encounter images of bodies being strangled and black women being sexually coerced by slave masters; the reader cannot easily evade a legacy of bodies being

10. Here Coates indirectly conjures up authors in the black radical tradition that have exposed how civilization/progress justifies "barbaric" actions against those bodies imagined as outside of civilization. See for instance, W. E. B. Du Bois, "The Souls of White Folk," in *DarkWater: Voices from within the Veil* (New York: Washington Square Press, 2004), 21–38; Aime Cesaire, *Discourse on Colonialism* (New York: Monthly Review Press, 1972).

twisted, hung, and punctured. These images, or scenes, of bodily violence produce a set of affects that cut against the grain of idealized notions like freedom and progress. Similarly, Coates's recurrent allusion to the "seized" black body prevents us from disentangling what Coates calls *the Dream*, or the fantasy of American plenitude and supremacy, from the black body's vulnerability to coercion and containment. If, as Coates points out, the Dream includes "perfect houses and nice lawns," this Dream "rests on our backs, the bedding made from our bodies" (11). In addition, if the Dream involves having one's rights and freedoms protected by the law, Coates suggests that the idea, and practice, of legal protection necessarily depends on a notion of a threat that needs to be regulated, monitored, and disciplined. As Coates puts it to his son, "The law did not protect us. And now, in your time, the law has become an excuse for stopping and frisking you, which is to say, for furthering the assault on your body" (17). Here Coates suggests that there is an insidious relationship between law, fantasy, and anti-blackness. The protection of the order of things, or the dream of order, largely depends on rendering black bodies disproportionately susceptible to State surveillance and violence. As Simone Brown describes, there is a long history of surveillance strategies, from policing black life under slavery to stop and frisk, that mark that black body as "matter out of place,"[11] or matter that needs to be put in its proper place. To use Mary Douglas's language, the imagined order of things relies on marking certain beings as dirt, as sources of incoherence and danger, sites of disorder that have to be eliminated or confined in some manner.[12] Black people, among other groups, have historically been conflated with that incoherent excess that troubles dreams of purity and coherence (blackness also attracts violent measures to contain that imagined excess). While most people might not *intend* racism, Coates argues that "a very large number of Americans will do all they can to preserve the Dream" (33), a Dream that sustains itself at the expense of black bodies.

Similar to Baldwin, Coates contends that "there exists, all around us, an apparatus urging us to accept American innocence at face value and not to inquire too much" (8). This apparatus—discourses, laws, rituals, images, cultural common sense—produces subjects that routinely disentangle

11. See Simone Browne, *Dark Matters: On the Surveillance of Blackness* (Durham, NC: Duke University Press, 2015).

12. On the relationship between order, purity, and dirt, see Mary Douglas, *Purity and Danger: An Analysis of Concepts of Taboo and Pollution* (New York: Routledge, 2002), 196–220.

freedom from violence, that subordinate loss and suffering to progress, that place a premium on American life (or those lives that more closely approximate the ideal American citizen), and that privilege the "infinite" possibilities of the future over the contradictions of the past and present. The Dream and presumption of innocence generate tendencies to imagine oneself as separate from and above the messiness that is history; it enables us to associate dirt and incoherence with other subject positions and communities, downplaying our own entanglements with, and vulnerabilities to, unpleasant realities and conditions. For Coates, this is not a predicament that is unique to (white) America. In fact, Coates warns, "Being black does not immunize us from history's logic or the lure of the Dream" (53). In addition, Coates suggests that the American dream/innocence myth is not necessarily exceptional; it is one powerful example of a human tendency to fabricate, perform, and cling to narratives that work to tame the unwieldy quality of life and history. Those, for instance, who respond to the legacy of colonization and anti-black racism by invoking nostalgic, idyllic images of a pre-colonial Africa are, according to Coates, beholden to a similar underlying fantasy as those tethered to the American dream. Both accept "comforting myths" that dissuade us from confronting "humanity in all its terribleness" (53). Of course, we should raise serious doubts about the possibility of eliminating myth, fantasy, and the need to mediate, and mitigate, the tragic. In fact, tragedy necessarily comes with its own myths and narratives. Yet we can say that, for Coates, the possibility of *something better* depends on interrogating our desires for wholeness and purity, and being more receptive to the terribleness that is our human condition—a terribleness that is exacerbated by all too human yearnings for wholeness and innocence.[13]

NEGATIVITY, STRUGGLE, AND THE AMBIVALENCE OF HOPE

It is tempting to interpret Coates's diagnosis of the racial order as a more accessible version of Afro-pessimism, a discourse that has recently gained traction in academic circles. Although I cannot do justice to this still emerging discourse in the space allotted, I take Afro-pessimism—especially in

13. Baldwin says something similar regarding the relationship between our attachments to myths and social practices, that while necessary, are organized around a denial of death and contingency. See Baldwin, "The Fire Next Time," 373.

its articulation by Frank Wilderson and Jared Sexton[14]—to be reimagining standard ways of thinking about race, recognition, and the human. While many strands of the black freedom struggle assume that the end goal of black strivings is recognition and inclusion within the sphere of the human, Afro-pessimists question this possibility—especially since the domain of the human is defined over against blackness. Riffing on authors like Frantz Fanon and Hortense Spillers, the pessimist contends that the sphere of recognition and law is made possible by simultaneously producing and excluding blackness, by permanently banishing blackness to a constitutive outside. As Wilderson puts it, "Whereas Humans exist on some plane of being and thus can become existentially present through some struggle for, of, or through recognition, Blacks cannot reach this plane."[15] Consequently, Hegel's Master/Slave relationship cannot be resolved and brought to a higher moment of reconciliation in the context of the black slave; for the pessimist, the struggle for recognition happens on a plane whose very coherence and legibility depends on the violent exclusion of the black/ abject body. Among the many implications of this Afro-pessimist formulation is ironically a potential rethinking of the pessimist-optimist binary.[16] Perhaps pessimism is always a relative term, or a term that makes sense in relationship to an object (pessimistic with respect to what?). More specifically, Afro-pessimism might understandably respond with a kind of despair to a social order structurally defined by anti-blackness, an anti-black apparatus that is often justified and mitigated by narratives of redemption and achievement. But this does not mean that the Afro-pessimist cannot think and imagine otherwise; it does mean however that any alternative imagination always emerges in the break, within the painful void that black pessimism inhabits.

Like the Afro-pessimist, Coates can be read as moving beyond the optimism-pessimism binary. Even though commentators like Brooks and

14. See for instance Frank Wilderson III, *Red, White, and Black: Cinema and the Structure of US Antagonisms* (Durham, NC: Duke University Press, 2010). Also see Jared Sexton, "The Social Life of Social Death: On Afro-Pessimism and Black Optimism," *In-Tensions* 5 (Winter 2011): 1–47.

15. Wilderson, *Red, White, and Black*, 38.

16. On the fluidity between Afro-pessimism and Afro-optimism (associated with the work of Fred Moten), see Sexton, "The Social Life of Social Death." Moten also seems to suggest that the binary (optimism-pessimism) does not really work or help to illumine the differences between his understanding of blackness and that of the Afro-pessimists. See Moten, "Blackness and Nothingness: Mysticism in the Flesh," *South Atlantic Quarterly* 112.4 (2013): 737–80.

Alexander accuse Coates of abandoning hope, it is not clear that *Between the World and Me* accomplishes this surrender. What is clear is that Coates refuses some of the dominating emblems and sources of optimism—such as the American dream, progress, and to some extent black Christianity.[17] This refusal does not preclude Coates from gesturing toward alternative sites of possibility. Moreover, Coates's tendency to tarry with antagonisms, without offering some kind of comforting resolution, might suggest that we should redefine the very notion of hope (or compel the regime of hope to give way to other kinds of desires, affects, and attachments that better register the complexities involved in being a black subject).

Coates seems to anticipate the charge that his book is an expression of despair. In a provocative passage that deals with themes of remembrance, redemption, and cynicism, he admonishes his son:

> You must struggle to remember the past in all its nuance, error, and humanity. You must resist the common urge toward the comforting narrative of divine law, toward fairy tales that imply some irrepressible justice. The enslaved were not bricks in your road, and their lives were not chapters in your redemptive history . . . Our triumphs can never compensate for [enslavement]. Perhaps our triumphs are not even the point. Perhaps struggle is all we have because the god of history is an atheist, and nothing about the world is meant to be. So you must wake up every morning knowing that no promise is unbreakable, least of all the promise of waking up at all. *This is not despair.* These are the preferences of the universe itself: verbs over nouns, actions over states, struggle over hope. (70–71)

In this passage, Coates suggests that remembrance must always watch out for narratives that readily instrumentalize the past, that turn the traumas and struggles of the past into an occasion for future redemption or deliverance. Similar to Walter Benjamin, Coates indicates that the past might make a claim on us (to remember, to mourn) but this "claim cannot be settled cheaply."[18] One of the ways in which the claims of the past are settled cheaply, or without much expenditure and self-loss, is by assuming that

17. On how Coates pushes back against a traditional civil rights, black church narrative, see Tressie McMillan Cotton, "*Between the World and Me* Book Club: Not Trying to Get into Heaven," *The Atlantic*, August 3, 2015, http://www.theatlantic.com/politics/archive/2015/08/between-the-world-and-me-book-club-not-trying-to-get-into-heaven/400271/.

18. Walter Benjamin, "Theses on the Philosophy of History," in *Illuminations*, trans. Harry Zohn (New York: Schocken, 1969), 254.

the achievements of the present compensate for the losses of the past. Triumphant accounts of history, as Benjamin and Coates suggest, relegate the dissonant quality of suffering and violence, that quality that disturbs and unsettles us, reminding us that historical forms of violence remain unresolved and part of the broken present. To say that the "enslaved . . . are not chapters in our redemptive history" is to refuse a logic that places suffering in an unfolding telos, that subordinates legacies of struggle to collective investments in a harmonious, unified future. This resembles Benjamin's claim that resistance and dissent are emboldened more by the "image of enslaved ancestors rather than that of liberated grandchildren."[19]

In opposition to traditional redemptive narratives, Coates underscores the beauty and permanence of struggle. Struggle is not despair—but perhaps is always being traversed and haunted by the inescapability of despair, moments of hopelessness that appear unproductive to the order of things. Coates links struggle to a Nietzsche-like ontology of becoming—the universe, perhaps indifferent to our goals and aspirations, is defined by flux, movement, and "verbs." Coates seems to invoke Nietzsche directly by calling the "god of history" an atheist, suggesting that even god is subject to the whims and vicissitudes of temporal existence. Even gods die (something to which Christian theologians, for instance, might not demur even if they read the implications of God's death differently). For Coates, every promise is breakable because human plans and projections cannot escape human mortality and contingency. What we thought was "meant to be" or the fulfillment of destiny is, for Coates, a product of contingent events, forces, and interactions. Thus he tells his son that he must "make peace with the chaos," (71) that he must accept the gap between our structuring frameworks of meaning and the unpredictable forces of the universe. But to make peace with the chaotic flow of life and history is to also acknowledge that we cannot remain in the space of utter chaos. In other words, humans will always need narratives, metaphors, and practices that make sense of, and manage, the disruptive movements of the universe.

In addition to the ontological and a/theological implications of struggle, we can also delineate the political consequences of Coates's affirmation of incessant striving. By affirming "verbs over nouns" and "actions over states," Coates is not necessarily denying the importance and necessity of goals within political movements. He is indicating that the goals of any struggle—redistributing wealth, ending police violence in working-class

19. Benjamin, "Theses on the Philosophy of History," 260.

black communities, ecological justice—should never become reified ends. What is more vital for Coates is the process of striving, the mobile and variegated struggles of black bodies against a resilient system defined by anti-blackness. By affirming movement and contestation over "states" and "destinations," Coates implies that there will always be tensions, antagonisms, constraints, and fissures that selves will encounter, qualities that are often diminished when we cling to unified ends and reconciled futures. By privileging "struggle over hope" Coates also indirectly responds to the Obama regime and the mantra of hope that accompanied Obama's ascendancy. Even though many resist the notion that Obama's presidency is the sign of a post-racial society, there remains a general assumption that the first black president is a kind of fulfillment of black freedom struggles, an assumption that flattens the complexities and richness of these struggles (not to mention the more radical possibilities opened up by black liberation movements). Therefore, Coates should be interpreted as refusing a certain kind of hope, the kind of hope attached to triumphant narratives of achievement that subordinate dissonance to harmony, or instability to order. In addition, the affirmation of movement and striving over hope suggests that hope might not be the best term to describe how people relate to the world's limitations and possibilities. In fact, Coates reveals that love, a difficult kind of love, describes his rapport with the world, potentially replacing the primacy of hope. In opposition to despair and cynicism, he tells his son, "I am not a cynic. I love you, and I love the world, and I love it more with every inch I discover" (71). Although Coates does not yet flesh out what this love of the world looks like, this invocation of love provokes several questions: Why does he contrast love with cynicism instead of hope and cynicism? What is the relationship between love, novelty, and discovery? What affects are directly associated with love that are less salient in the mantra of hope? Is it important that, in addition to this son, love's object is the world and therefore not limited to America, the nation-state, etc.? What are the limitations of a love ethic for political struggles and strivings or, inversely, how might a love ethic expand our conception of politics?

While these questions must be left partially unanswered, we can infer that Coates, as mentioned above, is explicitly thinking beyond the optimism-pessimism, or despair-hope, dichotomy. He refuses both a stance that would completely reject the world (as incorrigible, as devoid of possibility); he also refuses a stance that gazes to the future, expecting redemption, the resolution of the marks of anti-blackness, etc. Love is more immanent and in the moment than hope; love is conditioned by, and the condition of possibility, for discovery, intimacy, and openness others. And, as authors like Freud and Morrison show us, love is intertwined with anguish, hatred, painful pleasure, and disappointment. For Coates, love—as the alternative to pessimism—captures the complexities of our attachments, and repulsions, in a way that hope apparently cannot.

A close reading of Coates reveals that he is not against hope per se—since his inchoate appeal to love bears some resemblance to hope. Consequently, his book is not an experiment in despair.[20] As Tressie McMillan Cottom points out, because Coates departs from Obama's "audacity of hope" mantra as well as the rhetoric associated with sanitized versions of the civil rights movement, his "hope feels stark and brutal"[21] to many of his detractors. As Cottom suggests, what critics expect from Coates is some projected resolution, some kind of "benediction" that converts, for instance, the police killing of Prince Jones into something positive, upbeat, and encouraging. Coates's unwillingness to satisfy these expectations resembles Theodor Adorno's articulation of negative dialectics. Like Coates, Adorno's writings have been charged with being pessimistic and un-constructive. According to David Hoy, for instance, "Adorno's vision can be at times so strongly dystopian that it can enervate our ability to hope . . . his negative philosophy of history makes critical activity seem hopeless and directionless."[22] For Hoy, the labor of the negative, when stretched too far, undermines the aims of critical activity, especially the goal of directing our vision to more hopeful possibilities for living together.

Yet when thinking about the concerns of critics like Hoy, it is important to remember what Adorno is responding to as he performs the work of melancholy and dissonance in his writings. For Adorno, modern practices and imaginaries produce selves that are increasingly impervious to the pain and torment that they inflict on others. In *Dialectic of Enlightenment,*

20. Although recent scholarship by Robyn Marasco argues that despair, when reinterpreted through authors like Hegel, Adorno, Fanon, and Bataille, might actually generate possibilities for critical theory and political transformation. See Marasco, *The Highway of Despair: Critical Theory After Hegel* (New York: Columbia University Press, 2015).

21. See Cotton, "*Between the World and Me* Book Club: Not Trying to Get into Heaven"

22. David Couzens Hoy and Thomas McCarthy, *Critical Theory* (Oxford: Blackwell, 1994), 139. Richard Rorty makes a similar critique of Adorno. See Rorty, *Contingency, irony, and solidarity* (Cambridge: Cambridge University Press, 1989), 57.

Adorno suggests that the modern self progresses inasmuch as s/he dominates Nature, which is a signifier for those dimensions of the world that are opaque, unwieldy, and a threat to self-coherence and assurance. The need to master the recalcitrant aspects of the world (desire, affect, bodies historically associated with nature, suffering, non-human beings) for the sake of self-preservation requires a sense of distance or separation from these coherence-undermining facets of life. As Adorno points out, the modern self "detaches itself from sensuous experience in order to subjugate it."[23] To be sure, Adorno acknowledges that the modern self is not the source of its own contradictions; the modern subject is a product of multiple forces and circumstances, including the logic of capital, the primacy of instrumental reasoning, and the emergence of a culture industry that entices participants to desire uniformity, consensus, and effortless entertainment. For Adorno, these interlocking mechanisms work to form subjects with a diminished capacity to receptively engage the dissonance and torment that these mechanisms generate. As he writes in *Minima Moralia*, "It is part of the mechanism of domination to forbid recognition of the suffering it produces."[24] But Adorno, in other moments, suggests that the system of domination undermines itself. He claims, "The world is systematized horror, but therefore it is to do the world too much honor to think of it entirely as a system; for its unifying principle is division, and it reconciles by asserting unimpaired the irreconcilability of the general and particular."[25] For Adorno, no system is seamless; any system depends on division and antagonism, features that selves routinely experience even if we don't always call them by name.

Adorno contends that contemplation, art, and writing are activities that can render us more attuned to everyday modes of domination and suffering, and to the dissonance that is the "secret telos" of harmony.[26] For Adorno, an ethics of negativity is best described as "a consistent sense of non-identity."[27] The term "non-identity" here refers to the slippage between concepts and objects or what Kant might call the distance between things in themselves and things as they appear to our senses and understanding.

23. Theodor Adorno and Max Horkheimer, *Dialectic of Enlightenment* (Stanford: Stanford University Press, 2002), 28.

24. Adorno, *Minima Moralia*, translated by EFN Jephcott (New York: Verso, 2002), 63.

25. Adorno, *Minima Moralia*, 113.

26. See Adorno, *Negative Dialectics*, trans. E.B. Ashton (New York: Continuum, 1973), 149.

27. Adorno, *Negative Dialectics*, 5.

Beyond Kant's epistemology, Adorno's consistent sense of the non-identical responds to our tendency to explain away, or exclude, those aspects of experience that appear out of place, those facets of social life that refuse yearnings for coherence and unity. He claims, "What we differentiate will appear divergent, dissonant, negative for just as long as the structure of our consciousness obliges it to strive for unity: as long as its demand for totality will be its measure for whatever is not identical with it."[28] In other words, there is an antagonistic relationship between our striving toward unity, our compulsion toward identity, and our capacity to creatively engage alterity, ambiguity, and contradiction. (Things appear out of place the more we are invested in being settled. But since we cannot live without concepts, without endeavors to contain the impact of the non-identical, some degree of antagonism and danger will always accompany self–other encounters.)

In light of Coates's emphasis on the black body as a perpetual target of violence, it makes sense to broach the connection between negative dialectics and physical suffering. For Adorno, "It is the somatic element's survival, in knowledge, as the [unassuaged] unrest that makes knowledge move."[29] As I take it, Adorno is suggesting that the experiences and movements of the body—being assaulted and punctured or resisting the markings of power—both motivate our conceptual constructions and betray the limitations of the concept. While the body, as Judith Butler so famously argues, gains significance because of social norms and language, there is also something about the body—its materiality, its fleshliness, its vulnerability to pain and anguish—that cannot quite be rendered intelligible by our conceptual arsenal. The body connotes a kind of "unassuaged" excess that knowledge can never completely grasp or contain. This non-containability occasions a kind of hope; the work of the negative, which reflects the body's unrest, endeavors to enable suffering to speak. As Adorno puts it, "The smallest trace of senseless suffering in the empirical world belies all identitarian philosophy that would talk us out of that suffering."[30] As Adorno suggests, the cultivated inclination to forget or diminish the intensity of suffering is hopeless; the attempt to give a voice to everyday suffering creates a break, or an opening, within an order marked by pervasive indifference and cruelty. While identity-thinking, expressed in the demand for clarity, coherence, and the resolution of tension, draws us away from bodily suffering, negative

28. Adorno, *Negative Dialectics*, 5–6.
29. Adorno, *Negative Dialectics*, 203.
30. Adorno, *Negative Dialectics*, 203.

dialectics directs attention to dissonance and the gap between ideas and material, sensuous pain. In a manner that resembles Adorno's emphasis on the "somatic element," Coates reminds his son and the reader,

> In America it is traditional to destroy the black body—it is heritage. Enslavement was not merely the antiseptic borrowings of labor—it is not easy to get a human being to commit their body against its own elemental interest. And so enslavement must be casual wrath and random manglings, the gashing of heads and brains blown out over the river as the body seeks to escape. . . . There is no uplifting way to say this. I have no praise anthems, nor old Negro spirituals. The spirit and the soul are the body and brain, which are destructible. . . .The soul was the body that fed the tobacco, and the spirit was the blood that watered the cotton. (103–1)

Here we might question Coates's narrow understanding of terms like "spiritual" and "soul," especially since these tropes function in black religious and aesthetic practices in ways that accentuate physicality. We should, however, take Coates to be resisting tendencies to talk about slavery and anti-black violence in a manner that diminishes bodily anguish, that attempt to hover above the permeability and fragility of black bodies. Like Adorno, Coates pushes back against narratives and interpretive schemes that "would talk us out of suffering" with simplifying terms and tropes that devalue somatic experience.

CONCLUSION: HISTORY, FREEDOM, AND THE OPACITY OF PLEASURE|PAIN

As I have suggested, Coates's *Between the World and Me* offers an alternative way of thinking about America's racial history, especially in relationship to "grand narratives of freedom." By juxtaposing haunting images of black bodies undergoing the terror of slavery with contemporary incidents of State violence (Prince Jones, Eric Garner, Michael Brown, . . .), Coates shows the limitations of imaginaries that draw a straight line from slavery to freedom, that place black strivings on a linear trajectory of progress. Therefore, Coates's interventions resonate with Saidiya Hartman's endeavor to trace the afterlife of slavery in her magisterial text, *Scenes of Subjection*. Even though Hartman is primarily concerned about the contradictions experienced by formerly enslaved blacks in the period immediately following abolition, her arguments carry implications for how we think about freedom and liberty more generally. According to Hartman, the Emancipation was more of a shift and transition than a complete break from the past. In other words, the end of slavery—which for her was certainly a kind of achievement—initiated a shift toward a new regime of regulating black bodies. As Hartman puts it, "The complicity of slavery and freedom, or the very least, the ways in which they assumed, presupposed, and mirrored one another—freedom finding its dignity in this "prime symbol of corruption" and slavery transforming and extending itself in the limits and subjection of freedom— troubled, if not elided, any absolute and definitive marker between slavery and its aftermath."[31] The "complicity of slavery and freedom" points to Coates's insistence that modern notions of freedom and whiteness have been intertwined with desires to dominate, possess, and consume black bodies. The term "subjection of freedom" alludes to the ways in which Emancipation introduced new constraints to formerly enslaved selves—the debt-peonage system, sharecropping, vagabond laws, involuntary labor imposed on criminalized subjects, the terror of the Klan, etc. Blackness generated, and continues to generate, strategies of regulation and containment. Hartman contends that "the health and well-being of the nation depended upon the ability to control and contain the dangers posed by the presence of emancipated blacks within the body politic."[32] Insofar as blackness is imagined as a kind of contagion, the project of whiteness— always intertwined with fantasies of unconstrained freedom, the accumulation of property, and perhaps ironically the maintenance of order—will justify itself through violent efforts to contain, and eliminate, this danger.

Yet in a manner that is sometimes muted in Coates's *Between the World and Me*, Hartman draws attention to the practices and rituals that provided moments of burdened agency and anguished pleasure for captive black bodies. Whereas Coates seems to dismiss the spirituals as sources of false consolation in the face of bodily torture, Hartman—following Frederick Douglass's poignant description of slave songs— hears in these cries and hollers a kind of opacity and dissonance that cannot be contained within stable binaries—pain vs. enjoyment or anger vs. happiness. Taking seriously how slaves were often forced to perform happiness and levity in the coffle or on the auction block—to conceal pain and vulnerability—Hartman suggests that the slave songs formed a repertoire of survival tactics

31. Saidiya Hartman, *Scenes of Subjection: Terror, Slavery, and Self-Making in Nineteenth-Century America* (Oxford: Oxford University Press, 1997), 115.

32. Hartman, *Scenes of Subjection*, 161.

that enabled slaves to express anguish and a kind of vexed freedom. A key term for Hartman is "opacity," a term that registers the layered, ambivalent, and undetectable quality of black bodies in pain and enjoyment. As Hartman describes, opacity "enables something in excess of the orchestrated amusements of the enslaved . . . which similarly troubles distinctions between joy and sorrow and toil and leisure. For this opacity, the subterranean and veiled character of slave song must be considered in relation to the dominative imposition of transparency and degrading hypervisibility of the enslaved, and therefore, by the same token, such concealment would be considered a form of resistance."[33] Here Hartman is not only thinking of how slave songs such as "Wade in the Water" served as secret codes in preparation for escaping the plantation. She is also thinking of how the slave song merges affects that we usually separate for the sake of clarity and coherence—joy and pain, pleasure and anguish, intimacy and horror. There is something about the excessive quality of the slave's moan that refutes DW Griffith's depiction of happy, content slaves in *The Birth of a Nation* or Coates's assumption that the spiritual is disconnected from black flesh; at the same time, the opaque cry troubles accounts that would eliminate any traces of hidden pleasure, enjoyment, and intimacy within slave life. As Du Bois suggests, black strivings often occur within the veil/vale, in obscured spaces that are liminal and in-between, sites that potentially alter how we see, hear, and remember.

It is perhaps this sense of the opaque, as it relates to the interplay between pleasure and torment, or domination and momentary flight, that Coates could have developed more in *Between the World and Me*. At times, Coates seems to exclusively focus on the bodily pain experienced by black bodies, which is understandable in a cultural context that persistently denies the violence that it produces, consumes, and distributes. In addition, Coates appears to diminish the complexity of black aesthetic production when he associates praise anthems and Negro spirituals with simple consolation. Following Hartman's lead, we might think of the affinities, and discontinuities, between slave songs and the hip hop music that he celebrates in the text, affinities regarding opacity, excess, and the fraught relationship between beauty and horror, or anguish and intimacy. (By using the term "fraught relationship," I am thinking of how self-enjoyment often spells pain for other people; yet I am also thinking of how certain aesthetic practices render selves more pervious to the pleasure/pain nexus, defusing

33. Hartman, *Scenes of Subjection*, 36.

usual tendencies to bifurcate these affects.) Coates gestures toward this relationship between beauty and torment toward the end of *Between the World and Me*. Reflecting on his Homecoming to his Mecca, Howard University, Coates writes:

> That was a moment, a joyous moment, beyond the Dream—a moment imbued by a power more gorgeous than any voting rights bill. This power, this black power, originates in a view of the American galaxy taken from a dark and essential planet. Black power is the dungeon-side view of Monticello—which is to say, the view taken in struggle. . . . Even the Dreamers—lost in the great reverie—feel it, for it is Billie they reach for in sadness, and Mobb Deep is what they holler in boldness, and Isley they hum in love, and Dre they yell in revelry, and Aretha the last sound they hear before dying. We have made something down here. . . . Here at the Mecca, under pain of selection, we have made a home. As do black people on summer blocks marked with needles, vials, and hopscotch squares. As do black people dancing it out at rent parties, as do black people at their family reunions where we are regarded like the survivors of a catastrophe. As do black people toasting their cognac and German beers, passing their blunts and debating MCs. As do all of us who have voyaged through the death, to life upon these shores. (149)

As this passage indicates, we experience fleeting moments of joy and beauty that can be more powerful than a political victory, moments that temporarily interrupt the fantasies that structure and maintain the order of things. These moments of joy are related to the power of black aesthetic expression, songs and rhythms that perform, and induce, melancholy and anguish as well as celebration, love, and festivity. By invoking the traces of drug consumption (needles and vials) beside images of hopscotch and dance, Coates gestures toward the ways in which black bodies in places like Baltimore develop habits of play, pleasure, and laughter alongside, and in the midst of, imposed conditions of social death. Similarly, the juxtaposition of survival and catastrophe, and death and life, suggests that Coates's joyful vision of what black people have created "down here" is inseparable from struggle, pain, and loss. Similar to Hartman's elaboration of the opaque, Coates's sense of black joy is excessive; it points beyond itself and troubles ordinary distinctions between happiness and sadness, or sorrow and celebration.

In response to critics like Alexander and Brooks, we might say that hope for Coates is *beside* the point. Or to put it less bluntly, our attachment to traditional hope and freedom narratives reduces the array of affective possibilities involved in beautiful struggles. Perhaps Coates is not hope-*ful*—which does not mean that he is hopeless. Perhaps hope too frequently relies on a kind of postponement or deferral of desire. Perhaps hope will always leave us attached to the dream of fulfilling promises that were always already *broken*. While his relationship to hope is uncertain, we can say with some confidence that Coates affirms both the tragic and the festive dimensions of black living and striving. While he tends to focus on the former for understandable reasons, he does acknowledge that laughter, revelry, and pleasure are intertwined with, and bear the marks of, loss, torment, and struggle.